IMAGES OF WAUGH

A Cricketer's Journey

IMAGES OF WAUGH

A CRICKETER'S JOURNEY

FOREWORD BY RAY MARTIN

HarperSports

An imprint of HarperCollins*Publishers*

HarperSports

An imprint of HarperCollins*Publishers,* Australia

First published in Australia in 1998
by HarperCollins*Publishers* Pty Limited
ACN 009 913 517
A member of the HarperCollins*Publishers* (Australia) Pty Limited Group
http://www.harpercollins.com.au

HarperCollins*Publishers*
25 Ryde Road, Pymble, Sydney, NSW 2073, Australia
31 View Road, Glenfield, Auckland 10, New Zealand
77-85 Fulham Palace Road, London W6 8JB, United Kingdom
Hazelton Lanes, 55 Avenue Road, Suite 2900, Toronto, Ontario M5R 3L2
and 1995 Markham Road, Scarborough, Ontario M1B 5M8, Canada
10 East 53rd Street, New York NY 10032, USA

A C.I.P. record for this book is available from the National Library of Australia

Printed in Australia by Australian Print Group on 110gsm Matt Art

9 8 7 6 5 4 3 2 1
01 00 99 98

CONTENTS

ACKNOWLEDGMENTS

Special thanks to the members and management of the various
Australian cricket teams that I have toured with, and shared so many
fantastic experiences with over the years.

Thanks also to ...
Ray Martin for kindly contributing the foreword.
Trent Parke for his support and guidance.

The guys who used my camera to take the photographs in this book
in which I appear, most notably, Errol Alcott, who took most of these shots,
and Glenn McGrath, who calmly snapped the front cover photograph.

The people at Canon and Toyota, for their continued support.

Kylie Prats at Brevier Design, for her patience and professionalism.

Geoff Armstrong, for his help and dedication on this, our sixth book together.

www.stevewaugh.com.au

For news, scores, memorabilia and behind-the-scenes information on
Steve Waugh and Australian cricket, you can now visit the official Steve Waugh website,
at www.stevewaugh.com.au.

FOREWORD

BY RAY MARTIN

A picture is worth a thousand words. Or so the Chinese tell us.

Well, put a camera in Steve Waugh's hand and put him in India and a picture is worth more than that. Much more. I think it's inspiration ... not inflation! Until now, Steve's touch with his trigger finger has been sorely undervalued.

In recent years, he's shown he can craft some good cricket yarns between the covers of a book. We always knew that he could crack a ball superbly through the covers of a cricket ground. But frame and focus a 35mm camera and play a winning shot? I'd like to see that!!

Well, have a look. Steve Waugh has swapped the willow for the wide angle. The late cut for the light meter. And he's won 'Man of the Match' again.

On tour with Tubby and the team — part cavalcade, part camp. (With a little cross-dressing tossed in as spice.) Justin Langer in his baggy green cap and those nice, white scuffs ... a good look, for Mardi Gras!

But ... have a glimpse at Steve's portrait of the street seller he captions 'Sweet Smile'. A little girl with little to laugh about, you'd think. But the master batsman rewards her. Excuse the pun, but there's nothing negative about this picture. Click, click!!

A picture for your thoughts, lil' darling!! Immortality. For one moment. In a hot land where just living can be an art form. The art of survival, for some. She looks at the lens and smiles like the Mona Lisa.

This is a collector's album of smiles. Here an old man, smiling on the edge of a faded window frame. There a young man, with a crazy smile in the middle of a crowd crush. Michael Slater smiles when he sings, which seems to be all the time. Big Merv and beggars smile at Steve Waugh. There's the ritual of the 'Dummy-Spit Doll' smile. Cricketers who earn the dreaded 'Daktari' clobber *must* smile!! Losers have no choice.

Still, the sweet smile on the little girl lingers longest for me, I think.

They're all sharp and lasting images of a privileged life on the road. A crack in the door of an exclusive club that the rest of us can never join.

So, what next from Steve Waugh? A recipe book? The rules of social etiquette? *A Gentleman's Guide to the Fall Fashions*? Probably.

Ray Martin
August 1998

INTRODUCTION

BY STEVE WAUGH

As a young kid doing battle with my brothers in the backyard, listening to the mesmerising voice of the famous commentator Alan McGilvray and imagining I was Dougie Walters taking on the Poms, I never expected that one day my backyard dreams would become a reality. Indeed, my cricketing life has literally been a dream come true — one I hope many young kids of today aspire to.

Cricket has been extremely kind to me. Not only has it given me enormous enjoyment, but also comradeship and friendships to last a lifetime. And it has given me the opportunity to see the world and many of the world's different cultures.

There have been many highs and lows over the past 13 years playing for Australia, ranging from the tough, learning years of the mid-1980s to our memorable World Cup of 1987 and the upward curve the team began to take after the famous 1989 Ashes tour. I've played in countries as diverse as Denmark, USA, Hong Kong, Bermuda and Vanuatu, and at venues ranging from cricket's holy grail — Lord's — to a rundown athletics stadium in the Bronx, New York. I've met people from all walks of life, from the Queen to Mother Teresa, Nelson Mandela, Elton John and, no-less-importantly, the kids of Soweto and the leprosy sufferers of Calcutta. My cricket career has not only been a wonderful sporting experience, it has also been a real eye-opener for me as to what life might be all about. For that I'll be forever grateful.

During these years I've kept diaries on various tours and been lucky enough to have them published. As well as scribbling away, I've also clicked my way through over 2000 photographs that try to capture images that have caught my eye. Unfortunately, many of these are doomed to live a life at the bottom of a shoebox because I didn't centre the photo correctly or the light was coming from the wrong direction, but my theory has always been that if I take enough shots some of them have to turn out okay.

In publishing some of these photographs in this book I hope to let people see a different side to the players. So often, the public's perception of a Test cricketer's persona is determined simply by how he performs on the field rather than what he's like off the field. In fact, most international cricketers are just like the average person who watches the game. They enjoy their mates' company and a beer, and they can have a good laugh at themselves.

Some the images of the Indian sub-continent in *Images of Waugh* are quite confronting. But I'm always asked, 'What's it like to tour places such as India or Pakistan?' So I feel I have an obligation to show examples of the sights and situations that I've come across. The result is in no way meant to be downgrading, because there are, of course, many wonderful things to see in this part of the world — ranging from the awesome Himalayan mountain ranges to the exquisite beauty of the Taj Mahal — and so many of the people are warm and friendly. However, there is also poverty and disease, which Australians are not used to and sometimes can't relate to.

The images of the leprosy sufferers of Calcutta may seem grotesque and gruesome, but leprosy is a disease that is terribly misunderstood and its victims are still shunned by a large percentage of the Indian population. After visiting these people and then going to see the work being done in rehabilitation centres built to provide shelter and support for their children, I was drawn to the cause. Consequently, I am now a patron of the fund set up to help establish a girls wing at the Udayan home, a successful rehab centre in Calcutta.

The biggest problem with leprosy is the fact that people don't want to know about it and don't want to see it. By drawing attention to the struggle, I hope to play a small part in the battle to demonstrate that ordinary people can safely mix with leprosy sufferers, and that with education and money the disease can be eradicated altogether.

Throughout this book, I have stuck with the names of Indian cities as I found them. For example, Madras is referred to as Madras, as it was in 1986 when we played the second Tied Test in history, rather than Chennai, as it had formally become known when we played there in early 1998, and Bombay is always Bombay, rather than Mumbai. In contrast, the city of Guwahati in north-east India, where we played South Africa in a one-day international in 1996 and I came face to face with a good-looking giraffe at the local zoo, is called by its current name, rather than Gauhati, as it was once known. I trust in doing this I have not offended anyone. I guess, when it comes to the names of cities in foreign lands, I am a creature of habit.

I hope this book not only brings enjoyment, but also puts a different perspective on life as an international cricketer from the one the public is accustomed to seeing. And I hope it gives a laugh and maybe causes a gentle tear or two as well.

Enjoy the journey!

Steve Waugh
August 1998

For the children of Udayan.
May all your futures be filled with opportunities.

GLORY DAYS

THE AUSTRALIANS
NEW DELHI, 1998

A fantastic achievement by a team that certainly has had its fair share of detractors throughout the season. Beating India on their home turf in mid 40°C temperatures, despite the fact that many of the guys were feeling ill, showed that this bunch had certainly come of age at international level.

I believe this team will look back on this particular series, which we won after a slow start and after the Test team had been clearly outplayed in the first two matches of the three-Test tour, and say, 'That's when we gelled as a unit and became disciplined and tough in our mental attitude.'

At back (left to right): Mark Waugh, Michael Bevan, Mike Walsh (scorer), Ricky Ponting, Errol Alcott (physio), Adam Gilchrist (in front of Errol), Adam Dale, Darren Lehmann, Tom Moody. Front: Gavin Robertson, Michael Kasprowicz, Steve Waugh, Damien Fleming.

MARK TAYLOR AND GEOFF MARSH
PORT ELIZABETH, 1997

Maybe this is not my greatest photo, but it's certainly a great moment. The shot was taken seconds after Ian Healy hit the match-winning six to end the Second Test and give us the series in South Africa. This was one of Australia's greatest-ever, come-from-behind victories in my experience — led by Mark Waugh's 116 we made the 270 the South Africans had set us with two wickets in hand. This after the home team had been 0–83 in the second innings, effectively 0–184, at stumps on day two after making 209 and bowling us out for a miserable 108.

The joy and relief we all experienced after Heals' classic blow are clearly evident on Mark Taylor's face as he hugs Greg Blewett, while Swampy Marsh (centre) can't hide his delight.

RICKY PONTING
SYDNEY, 1998

With Ian Healy having been left out of the Australian one-day squad for the 1997–98 World Series, the honour of leading the team in the singing of 'Under the Southern Cross' was passed on to the passionate and strong-willed Ricky Ponting. It couldn't have been easy for Heals to choose his successor and the announcement was much anticipated by all the boys, with the final decision being a popular one.

Knowing how much it meant to Heals whenever we won a one-day series, the pressure was right on Punter to come up with an impressive debut performance after our excellent comeback victory over the South Africans in the World Series finals. But he didn't let anybody down with his repertoire, which included a nice little introduction full of observations about various efforts by the guys during our finals wins.

Here you can see him telling the lads about their feats, before the serious stuff begins. Let's hope we see Punter on top of that table many times in the future and, in particular, at Lord's in the English summer of 1999.

PARTY TIME

JOHANNESBURG, 1997

Immediately after achieving a great victory in the First Test of the series in South Africa, we jumped on a coach and headed for Sun City, some two-and-a-half hours from Jo'burg. Greg Blewett (far left) and I were in particularly buoyant spirits, having just posted the highest-ever Test-match partnership on South African soil — 385 for the fifth wicket.

This bus trip developed into one of the more memorable team journeys, with plenty of backslapping, wrestling and storytelling, aided by the deft hand of our barman, Andy Bichel (second from left). Bic's nip measurements would send any proprietor broke in no time at all.

The guys in the photograph are (left to right): Blewey, Bic, Paul Reiffel, S. Waugh, Jason Gillespie, Matthew Elliott, Justin Langer and Matthew Hayden.

MICHAEL SLATER, JUSTIN LANGER AND JASON GILLESPIE

JESMOND, 1997

Following our demolition of a fairly fragile Minor Counties XI at Jesmond, which is near Newcastle in north-east England, a whisper was about that we'd unearthed a new Lillee and Thomson-like combination. Well, that's what Slats and Lang thought anyway!

The truth of the matter was that they had certainly put some life into the late-afternoon proceedings. Before their appearance at the bowling crease, events on the field had most of the players and spectators yawning. The reason for this excitement was twofold. Firstly, both these specialist batsmen are actually frustrated fast men who get sick and tired of bowling endless overs in the nets without gaining any recognition when the real action begins. Secondly, our 12th man for the match, Jason Gillespie, ran a book for the day offering odds on such diverse things as how many sixes a player could hit, what the final total was going to be and so on. He also offered Langer at 10-1 and Slater at 7-1 about them taking a wicket.

For my money, Slats was pretty good value but Lang should have been 20s at least. Whatever, Dizzy's prices were sufficiently tempting for both to have a dabble on themselves.

As the Australians' captain for this fixture, I thought it only fair that I should give these boys a chance to stop the ridicule they regularly received in the nets. So I let them have a dip at the mediocre opposition.

First up, Slats (Lang's tag-team partner in midget wrestling) bamboozled the helpless No. 8 batsman with a beautifully disguised slower ball that lobbed safely into Paul Reiffel's hands at cover. Then, after coming in off a stupendous run, and with the crowd chanting 'Langer! ... Langer!! ...', Western Australia's answer to Willy Wonka's Oompa-Loompas found immediate success as the Minor Counties' captain, who'd scored 82, was caught on the mid-off fence as Michael Bevan intercepted a certain six.

The joy on both guys' faces was so obvious only a debut century could have matched it for sheer emotion. As for Dizzy?

He went straight for the kit bag to locate his wallet.

IAN HEALY

LEEDS, 1997

It's always a great sight to see Heals perched atop one of the team coffins, leading us into song after a game. After all, it means we have been successful.

Since taking over from David Boon, Heals has added his own unique brand of enthusiasm and challenges himself to make every team chorus better than the previous one. To do this, he knows which buttons to push, whipping the boys into a frenzy with a few 'pump-up' facts about the match — in this case, straight after the Fourth Test in 1997, at Headingley, he would have said something such as, 'Here's a drink for Herbie for that great dig! And one for Dizzy for the quickest spell I've ever seen and for taking seven of those pommy wickets!'

Matthew Elliott had scored a superb and very timely 199 in our only innings, while Jason Gillespie had finished the Test with nine wickets, seven of them (for 37) in England's first innings.

To make everyone that little bit more anxious and eager, Heals always keeps the team waiting until he's ready to perform. But once he does, the memory of his performance will soon be implanted in everyone's minds forever.

THE BAGGY GREENS
NOTTINGHAM, 1997

It was a couple of hours after the Ashes had been secured, but we were still high on adrenalin after such a barnstorming finish to the match that even surprised a few of us. I don't think those 'baggies' came off for quite a while! Certainly not while we stayed in the Trent Bridge dressing-room.

The lads in the photo are (in the dressing-room, left to right): Michael Kasprowicz, coach Geoff Marsh, Ian Healy, Shane Warne, Jason Gillespie, Michael Bevan and Steve Waugh. On the balcony are Greg Blewett, Justin Langer (complete with Aussie flag around his neck) and Paul Reiffel.

ONE IN ALL IN
NOTTINGHAM, 1997

I can still feel the moment, as we linked arms and belted out our team song with such passion and fervour that it still brings goosebumps out all over my body. These are the instances that are worth bottling, moments we wish every Australian could experience. But, unfortunately, you have to have a baggy green cap to be a part of it.

I hope you can notice the sensible ones drinking Coke.

MICHAEL BEVAN

ADELAIDE, 1997

Bevo flashes the pearly whites and rightly so, having just completed one of the most astonishing bowling performances by a 'part-timer' in the history of Test cricket. And he scored 85 not out as well! Considered by most as no more than a promising bowler, Bevo virtually single-handedly took down the might of the West Indies batting line-up with hauls of 4–31 and 6–82. This was a display of left-arm 'chinaman' bowling of the highest class, which ensured his name will be proudly etched forever on the honour board above his head.

MARK TAYLOR AND STEVE WAUGH
CANTERBURY, 1993

How sweet it was! To be able to take the cash of a touring journo!!

It was seen as a bold gamble by Taylor and Waugh, who both had a piece of the 20–1 AAP writer Patrick Keane was offering about Tubs taking two wickets during the entire tour (including all matches, even 'friendlies'). Such was the team's faith in our opening batsman's bowling ability, exactly no other member of the squad thought the odds were attractive.

However, a victim was had in our game against the Minor Counties in early July, and at this point my £400 return and Mark's £200 gain looked assured. But coming into the final two county games — against Kent at Canterbury and then Essex at Chelmsford — it seemed we'd be the ones opening up our wallets.

It was during our game against Lancashire in the final week of July that the plot had thickened. As per previous games, a huge banner, complete with the mocking words 'Mark Taylor Can't Bowl', had been erected by Mr Keane in the outer. Obviously spurred by this, and substantially helped by the fact he was captaining the side, Tubs grabbed the cherry and calmly said, 'I'm having a bowl.'

Within seconds, a simple, apparently harmless long hop was confronting a gleeful local lad, but in his eagerness to contemptuously swat it away, the batsman mishit it badly and lobbed a simple catch to the cover point fieldsman. But sadly that man moved the wrong way and then split the offering after the ball struck him between the hand and the elbow. Instantly, howls of laugher were heard emanating from the press box.

Needless to say, I was embarrassed and was also now sporting a painful lump where the ball had hit. And I was also fuming for letting the cash literally slip through my fingers.

Next day, Keane's banner blazed: 'Mark Taylor Can't Bowl ... and Steve Waugh Can't Catch!'

The gloves were off. But with only two county games and a Test remaining, and Mark scheduled to sit out the game at Chelmsford and very unlikely to ever talk Allan Border into letting him bowl in a Test match, it wasn't looking too promising. But, after tea on the final day of a three-day encounter, a stronger force took control as a gentleman by the name of Richard Davis of Kent strode to the crease.

Here we had a man in our midst who was still hurting from the ridicule of being spanked for six by Tim May during the 1989 Ashes tour (which won £600 for Tim Zoehrer, who had taken Dean Jones' offer of 30–1 about Maysie achieving his life-long goal on the tour). To put this feat in perspective, Maysie had earlier confessed that he'd never hit a six in any form of cricket. Not even in the backyard! It was something approaching a cricket miracle when his sweetly-timed 'hoick' sailed over mid-wicket and landed in the carpark.

Poor Davis was obviously still feeling the stigma of this calamity, as he again succumbed at the hands of the Aussies. A Taylor 'nude-nut' (there was nothing on it) snuck behind the batsman's legs as he attempted an ungainly sweep shot and the death rattle echoed around the ground. Joyous celebrations began, with high fives the order of the day, and Tubby punched the air in jubilation while a rather distressed Mr Davis trudged off in shame. To Patrick's credit, the cash was delivered via our 12th man at the conclusion of the over.

For most of our players, especially Mark and me, the remainder of the game was a major anti-climax.

GREG BLEWETT

JOHANNESBURG TO SUN CITY, 1997

One of the pin-up boys in the Aussie side. Perhaps we should muster up enough of them for a crack at a calendar!

THE AUSTRALIANS
ADELAIDE, 1997

Breaking the phenomenal West Indies' unbeaten streak in Australia–Windies Test series, which had extended back 17 years, in the Caribbean during the '95 tour was a memorable achievement for all those involved. However, it would have been tarnished if we hadn't followed it up with a repeat performance on our home soil in 1996–97.

By then, it was more than 20 years since we had toppled the West Indians in Australia, so you can see why it was so significant for us and why the celebrations were especially animated after we clinched the series at the Adelaide Oval. Heals, as he always does, excelled himself atop the table and it was great to have David Boon (far right of the photo on page 15), who had been flown in to Adelaide to be a part of the festivities, there with us despite the fact he had retired the season before.

The move to bring Boonie to the scene of our triumph was a gesture from management that recognised the contribution over many summers of a great Australian player who had never been part of a team that had conquered the West Indies in Australia. It demonstrated in some small way how we all realised that he deserved to take some of the credit for the team's victory.

One other feature of this image is the fact that Glenn McGrath (far right) is already one step ahead of the rest of the lads — he's sporting a shirt already soaked in beer. Knowing Pigeon, he'll be responsible for plenty of mayhem once the real action begins. And as it appears that Heals has just completed this rendition of 'Under the Southern Cross', I'd reckon the party is just about to start. Warney (closest to camera) and Lang (immediately to Pigeon's right) certainly think so.

BRENDON JULIAN
NOTTINGHAM, 1997

Moments before the Ian Healy-led team song, an early-morning (Australian time) call was made to give the lads who had been forced through injury to go home early a chance to join in the celebrations. In this case, it was BJ who got Adam Gilchrist on the line and let him be part of the victory, which hopefully in some small way alleviated his disappointment at not being with us in person.

The two gentlemen to BJ's right are Justin Langer (in baggy green) and Michael Kasprowicz.

WHO ARE THESE MEN?

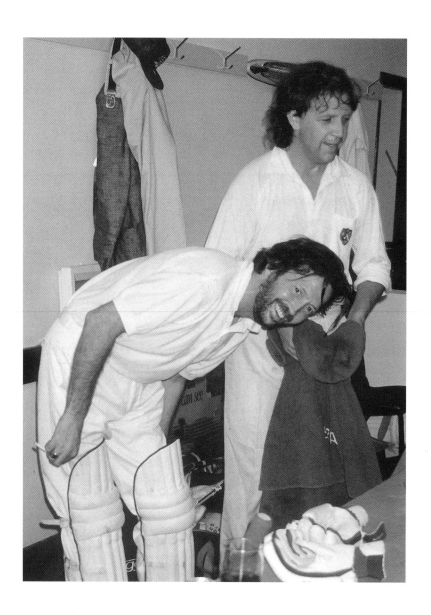

ERIC CLAPTON
SOUTHAMPTON, 1988

Playing county cricket, as I did for Somerset in 1988, was an eye-opening and career-enhancing experience. One of the benefits of being on this professional circuit was being able to meet other prominent sportspeople and celebrities from a variety of fields.

As part of the efforts to raise funds for 'SportAid', a charity that had been set up to try to help the children of the world, I played in a match that also featured music legends Eric Clapton and Bill Wyman. During the play, I lent my pants, shirt and protective gear to Australia's own Jimmy Barnes, who also graced the field. Well, he did briefly, having his stumps shattered by the second ball he faced. But this wasn't too surprising, as he did look a bit the worse for wear after his concert the previous evening.

THE AUSTRALIANS
LAHORE, 1994

This photo was taken during the awards ceremony for the team's 'facial hair growth' contest during our tour of Pakistan. Is that Shaggy from 'Scooby Doo' to Michael Slater's left? And how come former England captain Mike Gatting (far left) got a run in the team photo?

The guys in the photo are (left to right): Bob Simpson, Justin Langer (in front), Steve Waugh, Ian Healy (at back), Damien Fleming, Jo Angel, Michael Slater (in front), David Boon, Glenn McGrath (in front), Tim May, Gavin Robertson, Craig McDermott (in front), Michael Bevan.

GREG DYER

BOMBAY, 1987

No-one knew our keeper Greg Dyer (above right) was going to catch up with his long-lost twin brother during our 1987 World Cup tour of India and Pakistan. Not even Greg himself!

The 'reunion' occurred during a cocktail party at a Bombay hotel, when the drinks waiter had us all doing a double take after he offered the lads a cleanser or two. Needless to say, GD took a hammering over the next few days about his family's well-kept secret.

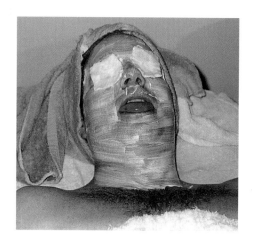

IAN HEALY

JOHANNESBURG, 1994

Heals required a bit of enticement before he succumbed to this facial in Jo'burg during the '94 tour of South Africa. The impact of prolonged hours in the sun and many long and arduous plane flights convinced our keeper he was in desperate need of some rejuvenation. That didn't quite happen, but I certainly enjoyed being there to capture the proceedings on film and expose a softer side of this tough, seasoned campaigner.

STEVE WAUGH, IAN HEALY, SHANE WARNE AND PAUL REIFFEL

CHRISTCHURCH, 1993

We must have been bored during this New Zealand tour. What we had done was go out in search of a new suit each, to be worn as part of the celebrations after a team victory. In this case, we'd just beaten the Kiwis by an innings and 60 runs, and initially the move up in the fashion stakes went down well. But gradually cracks began to develop in the plan, especially after the 'Paul Reiffel' lookalike, whom we called 'The Joker', decided his fashion statement needed a change in direction.

For the life of me, I can't remember the identity of the bloke in the jeans who owns the classy pair of shoes.

SHANE WARNE
MANCHESTER, 1993

Like a lot of cricketers, Warney likes to feel nice and relaxed going into a Test match. Part of his pre-game ritual, as it is for most of us, is to visit the hairdressers.

The trademark blonde locks are being well catered for here, in preparation for the First Test of the 1993 Ashes tour, at Old Trafford. Whatever shampoo was used must have worked, as Shane finished the match with eight wickets, including one of his most famous — Mike Gatting, bowled by an amazing leg-break that just happened to be the first ball Shane ever bowled in Test cricket in England.

NERDS V JULIOS
MANCHESTER, 1993

Not long after we arrived in England for the '93 Ashes tour, we divided ourselves into two groups: the 'Nerds' and the 'Julios'. Which team you made depended on your looks, dress sense and use of hair gel — or lack thereof. Into the Nerds went David Boon, Allan Border, Ian Healy, Merv Hughes, Tim May (captain), Paul Reiffel, Bob Simpson, Mark Taylor, Steve Waugh and Tim Zoehrer, while the Julios included Matthew Hayden, Wayne Holdsworth, Craig McDermott, Damien Martyn, Michael Slater, Shane Warne and Mark Waugh and were led by physio Errol Alcott.

First up, in Worcester, we gave the pretty boys a lesson at touch football. Then, a few weeks later, we set off to a tenpin bowling alley in Manchester, where we hoped to take a 2–0 series lead.

On the morning of the big game, it was decided we needed an appropriate team uniform, so Heals and I headed off with Maysie to try to find the right gear. And as we prepared for the confrontation, we thought we'd dressed ourselves pretty well. But on the night, while our bowling

techniques might have been impressive, both our outfits and the final score left a lot to be desired.

Looking back on the tussle, I firmly believe Merv (right) was the cause of our defeat. This was doubly frustrating because we had all believed he was going to be our trump card. But instead of concentrating on how many pins he could blast over, the big fella was more interested in seeing how far he could lob the ball down the alleyway. Such a strategy made for an enormous thud but little accuracy, though it did cause plenty of laughs and got us more than one curious glance from the adjoining lanes.

Not that we needed any extra attention, resplendent as we were in our highly fashionable £1.50 shirts and £1 sunglasses.

On page 37 is the historic photograph of the two teams together, just moments before the beginning of play. Left to right: Simpson, Healy, Hayden, Hughes, S. Waugh, Slater, May, Zoehrer, McDermott, Holdsworth, Julian, M. Waugh.

SHANE WARNE
ARUNDEL, 1993

Warney rehearsing his appeal, a week into his first Ashes tour. By the time he was finished with the Poms, having taken 34 wickets in the six Tests (the most ever by an Australian spinner in an Ashes series in England), practice had made perfect.

MATTHEW HAYDEN AND JASON GILLESPIE
PORT ELIZABETH, 1997

One of our greatest Test-match wins was followed by some sensational post-match entertainment provided by two of our players ...

Leading up to the Test, Haydos, who is a nature lover, kept using the analogy of Australia being the hunter and South Africa being the hunted. We, he insisted, were hungrier than them for the victory. As things turned out, his words were quite prophetic, and to show his gratitude for the way the team had proved him right, he decided to celebrate with a mock hunt and kill.

To help with the re-enactment, he enlisted the services of Dizzy Gillespie. No expense was spared, with sun cream and vegemite substituting for war paint. And such was the passion of their stalking in the make believe bushes that terror was struck into the mesmerised lads as this fearsome duo went searching in earnest for some South African scalps. After a good 15 minutes of unique theatre, Haydos and Dizzy had succeeded in snaring their victims, finishing in style by rolling around the beer-soaked floor to the deafening applause of the entire squad.

You had to be there! It was great!!

WHO ARE THESE MEN?

GEOFF MARSH
ROYAL PORTRUSH, 1997

Geoff Marsh, marooned in one of the world's biggest bunkers, at Royal Portrush. The course is located on the northern coast of Northern Ireland, about an hour from Belfast, and its unforgiving nature is perfectly captured by the names chosen for two of its toughest holes — 'Calamity Corner' and 'Purgatory'. Royal Portrush hosted the British Open in 1951, the only time the tournament has been held outside mainland Britain.

From parts of the course you can gaze out at beautiful sandy beaches, rolling green countryside and the extraordinary Giant's Causeway. However, from where our intrepid coach found his ball you can see nothing but sand.

MERV HUGHES

BIRMINGHAM, 1993

A photograph taken during our celebrations in the Edgbaston dressing-rooms after we'd won the Texaco Trophy one-day series on the '93 Ashes tour.

Merv was always great value, whether on the field, where he always gave 100 per cent, or off it, where he was always keeping the squad's spirit high with his unique blend of humour and personality. Here is one of the big man's party favourites — the crushed beer can to the head, John Belushi style, backed up by the full one at the ready, to be spurted at the nearest team-mate, and the 'Sumo' impression courtesy of the wrap-around towel.

DAVID BOON, TIM MAY, GAVIN ROBERTSON AND MICHAEL BEVAN

LAHORE, 1994

Here are the four winners of the Australians' facial hair contest, which was conducted through the final four weeks of our tour of Pakistan. The award for the 'thickest growth' went to Boonie, who had been an odds-on favourite from the start. Maysie won the 'best goatee' trophy, mainly through a lack of decent competition. Robbo won the 'encouragement award' — he'd been trying for a full beard and this was all he had to show for his efforts.

But Bevo was judged best of all. We reckoned he made the fiercest of the Hell's Angels look tame!

MERV HUGHES

LONDON, 1993

Most of the lads reckon that any publication that needs a 'mug' shot will always use the worst one that was taken, so who could blame Merv for giving the snapper the look that they'd be after? It must be said that, given we had just stumbled off a plane from Australia, Merv's look was in keeping with how we felt. It wasn't quite the time to be shoved in front of some bright lights and told to smile.

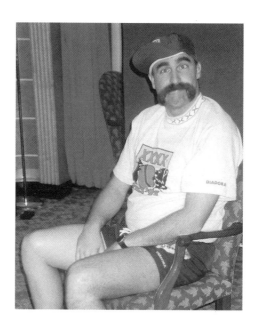

SHANE WARNE
KINGSTON, 1995

This photograph was taken not long after I'd made exactly 200 against the West Indies in the fourth and deciding Test, at Sabina Park in Jamaica, in 1995.

Warney has just talked me through the story of his second-ball duck. He'd come to the wicket with the score on 8–522, after Paul Reiffel and I had added 73 for the eighth wicket. I was 195 not out, and Shane, being the great team man that he is, was desperately keen to be at the crease when I reached 200. But if you look closely at the photo you can see the reason for his immediate dismissal.

As you can see, the top of the grill is in a very poor position, directly in line with Warney's line of vision. Of course, it shouldn't be. It was in this state because it had been tossed onto the ground during the previous tour match and Shane hadn't stopped to check if it was damaged. He just put it in his kitbag and took it to Sabina Park. Unfortunately, the next time he pulled it out was in the middle of the Test match when he was required in the middle.

As everybody knows, it's hard enough facing the Windies quicks without any extra handicaps.

JUSTIN LANGER
NOTTINGHAM, 1997

The great thing about Lang is his commitment and love of the team. Even though he didn't play a Test on tour, he was always there celebrating our wins until the revelry was no more. On this occasion, we all had good reason to party, as this was the day we won a record fifth straight Ashes series, so perhaps Lang can be excused for the cross-dressing look. But it must be said that the shoes (borrowed from Greg Blewett's then fiance, now wife, Jodie) are a nice touch, blending nicely with the Aussie flag and the baggy green cap.

STEVE WAUGH
JOHANNESBURG, 1994

The dreaded 'Chips' doll, which was awarded to the team member who put on the biggest dummy spit of the week. It's an appropriate 'trophy', because he has a thumb that fits neatly into his mouth.

Like the dreaded Daktari, Chips is another embarrassing team award that brings much anguish to the recipient. He must be taken everywhere by his 'owner' and is guaranteed to ignite a conversation with a stranger. He's also extremely awkward to carry, but by the end of the South African tour he was a much loved member of the squad.

TIM MAY
LEEDS, 1993

Maysie in heaven after our decisive win at Headingley on the highly successful 1993 Ashes tour.
I don't think Tim was responsible for all the empties, but he would have been a contributor. In truth,
the contents of 90 per cent of the crushed cans would have ended being sprayed onto the roof or
splashed onto the floor during the team's unique celebration song.

MARK TAYLOR AND MERV HUGHES
GOLD REEF CITY, 1994

On a rare day off on our South African tour of 1994 we spent the afternoon at the Gold Reef City amusement park, which is located just outside Johannesburg on what was once a thriving diamond mine. Now being down a disused mineshaft can be a little intimidating in itself, but this view of Tubby and Big Merv made the atmosphere doubly terrifying.

TIM MAY
NEW PLYMOUTH, 1993

On just about every Australian cricket tour I've been on, we've established two committees for the squad's benefit. One is the fines committee, the other looks after the social side of things and both play an important role in helping to enhance team spirit and the togetherness of the lads — by having a few laughs at your mate's expense.

In what has become a tradition, the social taskforce is able to order an individual to don an outfit so horrific that the wearer will have to bear the brunt of many a sideways glance, constant ridicule and snide laughter whenever the outfit is worn.

The winner of this award, called the 'Daktari' after a particularly distasteful number bought by Tom Moody and me during an Australian XI tour of Zimbabwe in 1991, can earn it by messing up in any number of ways on tour. This could be done by being continually late for the bus, by a temper tantrum in the nets, embarrassing acts, stupid comments, anything that a team vote decides is deserving of public humiliation on a chosen night in the following week.

By 1993, the Daktari had been doing the trick for a couple of years, but as members of the social committee during the '93 New Zealand tour, Maysie and I set off into town in search of an outfit even worse than the Daktari, something even Tubby Taylor wouldn't wear. Tim, as always, sniffed out a possible lead and we strolled into a Salvation Army store in New Plymouth, where we knew immediately that we'd hit the jackpot. In front of us were the motleyest collection of safari suits, bell bottom trousers and jumpers and other items of clothing that must have been previously owned by either chronic attention-seekers or people born colour blind.

By the time Maysie had tried on this combination (his fifth of the day!) a crowd had gathered in much the same way a busker attracts people on the sidewalk. The people privileged to see this little sideshow finally broke down, laughing, when Tim adopted a 'catwalk' pose, lurched up against the makeshift cubicle door. This was exactly the response we wanted. We knew we'd found our outfit. But, sadly, the strides had only a 32 waist and therefore would have been too small for at least half the team.

So off we went to continue our search for the right outfit and a few more laughs.

MICHAEL SLATER
LEEDS, 1997

No, it's not Willy Wonka or Crusty the Clown. It's Australia's dashing, debonair opener Michael Slater belting out one of his favourite Bon Jovi numbers atop the dressing-room table, as the celebrations continue after the Fourth Test had been won. The wig came courtesy of one of the Canberra Raiders football contingent, who had so enthusiastically shown their support from the Headingley outer during the last day's play.

A Cricketer's Lot

David Boon's Fan Club

Bermuda, 1995

Boonie's reputation had obviously preceded him. During our brief stopover on the way home from winning the Frank Worrell Trophy, we checked out all the island had to offer. I'd be very surprised if this particularly generous example of hospitality wasn't taken up by our prized No. 3.

And by a few of his team-mates!

MERV HUGHES
SUN CITY, 1994

It was either buy back the balls we'd lost over the previous five horrendous holes, or the game was over. The bad form of the foursome of Hughes, Warne, May and S. Waugh was a direct result of the whiplash we'd all suffered at the second. In pursuit of our collectively wayward tee shots, we'd torn off in our motorised golf carts doing the usual tricks — darting in and out, edging as close to each other as possible without touching wheels, and so on. It was during a steep decline that the Hughes/Warne mobile opened up a handy lead, to the point that Maysie and I realised the race had been lost. So we decided to take in the panoramic views.

Bad move. The lead cart had, unbeknown to us, ground to a halt. What they wanted was to carry on the skylarking. The result was a shuddering clash of plastic and metal that jolted our heads violently back and forth and ended any chance of a competitive round.

By the fifth, we were terrible. From there our golf went to atrocious, and a halt was called approaching the ninth green after our newly re-acquired batch of balls had once again disappeared into the African scrub.

STEVE WAUGH AND JUSTIN LANGER
GIANT'S CAUSEWAY, 1997

The Irish claim the Giant's Causeway, a rocky promontory on the northern coast of Northern Ireland, as the eighth natural wonder of the world. Many would say rightfully so, as it is a sight that demands your attention through its beauty and uniqueness ...

On my left in this photograph was a man who was creating his own little piece of folklore. During our dizzy celebrations in the early morning after claiming the Ashes at Trent Bridge, Lang, Slats and I had made a pact to keep our green baggies on for the whole of the Irish leg of our tour. Four days in all. Now anyone who has ever had a whiff of a felt cap saturated in beer knows it isn't going to be easy to put it on your dial, let alone keep it there for another 96 hours. Commonsense and the constant looks of bewilderment from others got the better of Slats and me, but Lang powered on through the discomfort, the smell and the insults to record a feat that may never again be seen, let alone attempted. I think one can only admire him for that.

ANDY BICHEL
CAPE TOWN, 1997

This man should definitely have a contract with Chesty Bonds! For the likes of S. and M. Waugh, Taylor and Warne, it's an absolute 'no no' to sit next to Bic in the dressing room, as the comparison between physiques is embarrassing.

This photo was taken on a day when a few of the boys were lucky enough to be taken cray fishing. It turned out to be one of the most memorable days off on the tour.

MICHAEL SLATER
DURBAN, 1994

Slats, as ever, keen to show off the rewards of working out in the gym. In fact, Slats' generation has a lot to answer for, because they have to be held accountable for today's increased fitness regimes, due to their rippling physiques that require daily attention through a succession of workouts. Their dedication means, of course, that we older players have to go along with them.

STEVE WAUGH, TIM MAY, PAUL REIFFEL AND GLENN McGRATH
SUN CITY, 1994

Four Nerds at Sun City, fresh from — can you believe it! — a game of Putt Putt!

JUSTIN LANGER
LONDONDERRY, 1997

On the two occasions I've been to Ireland, during the Ashes tours of 1993 and 1997, the team has had a brilliant time enjoying the hospitality and the beautiful scenery. On our last trip we journeyed to Londonderry, just outside Belfast, where the locals took us out to their well-kept-secret locations to fish for the famous Scottish salmon. Unfortunately, either they dudded us or we just had an off day because Lang's prized catch was our only success for the day. I reckon this fish must have been a kamikaze pilot in a previous life.

GEOFF MARSH
COLOMBO, 1996

On a rare day off during our time in Sri Lanka in August–September 1996, Swampy, Pigeon and I decided to try a bit of sightseeing. However, because of the security concerns the locals had about our tour, this wasn't an easy thing to organise.

The problems had emanated from Australia's decision not to play our scheduled match against Sri Lanka in Colombo during the 1996 World Cup, which had been played in February and March. We worried about a backlash when we did journey there five months later and this fear, combined with our Board's insistence on tight security, meant that for much of the tour we felt like prison escapees, such was the police presence around us.

To give you an example of the paranoia that existed during the tour, on game days decoy buses left before us, with curtains closed, on alternative routes to the ground, while we set off in a different direction, with curtains also closed and six commandos with automatic rifles at the ready guarding us in the aisles.

This is probably why Swampy sported such a huge grin as he caressed his new-found friend, while our baggageman of many trips to Sri Lanka, Mr Siripala, looks on.

This man has to be, pound for pound, the strongest man on earth. He regularly lifts two cricket coffins at once with arms that make Olive Oyl look like Rod Marsh. Siripala has become so well liked and respected by all the Australians that when we discovered he was living in a shed with his wife, daughter and mother-in-law, with no future plans to build on his block of land because his wage was so pitiful, we decided to help. Donating $US1500 to him at the end of the tour allowed him to start building the four walls of his house.

CARL RACKEMANN

KINGSTON, 1995

'Mocca' Rackemann picked up these souvenirs when we visited the resort town of Ochio Rios, two hours from Kingston and made famous by the waterfall scene in the Tom Cruise movie 'Cocktail'. The reaction of the boys to Mocca's buys was at best lukewarm, but compared to the problems he was going to have getting the goods through Customs, what we thought of his purchases was the least of his problems.

GLENN McGRATH, DARREN BERRY, STEVE WAUGH AND SHANE WARNE

LONDONDERRY, 1997

Our mini-break on the Ashes tour in Northern Ireland was a welcome one, as it took us away from the cricket grounds and allowed us to pursue other sporting activities. This quartet started out rather promisingly but faded on the back nine — the eventual victory to Waugh and McGrath came courtesy of a six on the par-three 18th.

We'd nearly lost our spin maestro early on when his golf cart sped out of control down a steep slope. He eventually came to a halt, but only after unintentionally executing a full 360, courtesy of a heavy foot on the dewy surface.

THE AUSTRALIANS

NOTTINGHAM, 1997

The 1997 Ashes team was sponsored by Coca-Cola, who also sponsor the AFL, so as a cross promotion they asked us to nominate our favourite footy team so they could outfit us with a jumper each. Good idea in theory, but the English summer doesn't really suit these sleeveless numbers.

Second from left, wearing the colours of his beloved St Kilda, is Warney telling the lads that if they want to look muscular in the publicity shot that was about to be taken we needed to lock our arms together in such a way that the knuckles were pushing out the biceps, to give us that extra bit of definition. As you can see, the plan worked quite nicely for Slats and Blewey, but Heals clearly needs a couple of extra sets of knuckles.

The players are (left to right): Paul Reiffel (Richmond), Shane Warne (St Kilda), Ray Phillips (the Australians' reserve wicketkeeper on the 1985 Ashes tour and sponsor's liaison officer in 1997; Collingwood), Matthew Elliott (almost totally obscured behind Ray; Collingwood), Justin Langer (West Coast), Michael Bevan (obscured at back; Hawthorn), Michael Kasprowicz (standing behind Lang; Brisbane), Ian Healy (Brisbane), Brendon Julian (standing behind Heals; West Coast), Ricky Ponting (North Melbourne), Greg Blewett (Adelaide), Mark Taylor (Hawthorn), Glenn McGrath (Sydney), Michael Slater (Sydney), Darren Berry (St Kilda).

Jason Gillespie (Adelaide) and Mark Waugh (Sydney) are hidden at the back of the group, between BJ and Pigeon.

SHANE WARNE 'FAN'
JOHANNESBURG, 1994

This little bloke ran after the team bus flashing this placard on the morning of the First Test, at the Wanderers Ground. He sure seemed anxious to get Warney's attention.

I'm not really sure of the meaning behind the message, but I presume it wasn't meant to be complimentary.

DESERT DANCING
DUBAI, 1998

During one of our days off during the triangular series in Sharjah we headed into the sands of Dubai for a desert BBQ. Dinner was preceded by a four-wheel drive trek up and down the dunes, and before the evening's lamb and beef had been well done this particularly shapely woman gave us a lesson in belly dancing. Moods (Tom Moody, behind the belly dancer) rated himself highly in the rhythm department, while Harvs (Ian Harvey, far left) got his money's worth from the sidelines.

The other 'dancers' are (from left to right): Shane Warne, Damien Martyn, Adam Dale and Michael Kasprowicz.

MICHAEL SLATER, STEVE WAUGH AND JUSTIN LANGER
BERMUDA, 1995

After completing the greatest Test victory of our careers in Jamaica, to win the series against the West Indies, we jetted off to Bermuda for a couple of friendlies against the locals and some much-needed rest and relaxation.

We were, though, still in the mood for records and set off to try to smash the previous mark for the most expensive team dinner ever ordered. The bill for team dinners is handled, of course, by the Australian Cricket Board.

The restaurant we chose had in the previous 12 months been voted one of the 50 finest in the world and we began by ordering only the best French champagne, which proved perfect for washing down the lobsters and succulent fillet steak that followed. The girls were treated to roses while afterwards the boys allowed themselves the luxury of a 'havana', if they so desired.

To begin proceedings, Messrs Slater, Waugh and Langer had opted for the fabled 'beluga caviar'. At $US75.00 per ounce, we certainly wouldn't have been smiling if we'd had to pay for it. And, I can assure you, we weren't smiling after we tasted it!

THE HOME OF GOLF
ST ANDREWS, 1997

We're outside the clubhouse, but someone got the dress instructions horribly mixed up, which explains the assortment of outfits ranging from Lang's coat and tie to the assortment of t-shirts, tracksuit tops and sleeveless sweaters.

Throughout this debacle, Heals shone like a beacon and was dressed impressively enough to be chosen in the top 10 best-dressed men for the year by one of Australia's leading women's magazines.

It's always a highlight to get a round in at St Andrews during an Ashes tour, but the chance to play the famous Old Course was denied us this time. However, undaunted by this setback, the lads dashed across to the famous 17th, the 'Road Hole', at the end of the day and played one of golf's greatest par fours before any of the course inspectors could spot them.

Back row (left to right): Matthew Elliott, fitness trainer Steve Smith (standing in front of Elliott), Michael Kasprowicz, Brendon Julian, Paul Reiffel, Glenn McGrath, Michael Bevan, Mark Waugh, Ian Healy, coach Geoff Marsh. Front row: Justin Langer, Darren Berry, Michael Slater, Greg Blewett, Ricky Ponting, manager Alan Crompton, scorer Mike Walsh, Steve Waugh.

MICHAEL SLATER

LONDON, 1997

The whisper was that Harry Connick Jnr was in town. Well, that's who Slats said he was impersonating when he put on this impromptu performance in the corridor of the team's hotel. Our opener's music could best be described as very 'raw' with plenty of energy, in much the same vein as the Sex Pistols.

SHANE WARNE
NOTTINGHAM, 1997

While in the late Harold Larwood's former hometown, Shane and I visited the over-100-year-old bat factory of our sponsor, Gunn & Moore, to see some handmade bats being crafted to the point where they are ready to be sold. Most batsmen go through three or four bats in a year, but Warney changes them as often as he eats Margherita pizzas, always in search of that once-in-a-career 'belter'.

INDIAN SUMMERS

SUPERMAN
CALCUTTA, 1998

Here is India's version of the man of steel, straight from the telephone booth and draped in an Indian flag, putting the heat on the Aussie contingent at Eden Gardens. In the end his words were quite prophetic, as we tumbled to a very heavy defeat.

IMAGES OF WAUGH

GIRAFFE
GUWAHATI, 1996

It's hard enough to counter a fast bowler's glare during the heat of battle. That was my first thought when I copped this fixed, silent stare at Guwahati Zoo in the far north-east of India. The next thing I thought was that Adam Gilchrist would be proud of the bloke's peepers!

This photograph was taken on an Australian cricket tour unique for the fact that we didn't win a single game.

SNAKE CHARMER
OUTSIDE THE AMBER FORT, RAJASTHAN, 1996

The much talked about, almost mythical battle between the lethal cobra and its nemesis, the mongoose, is always worth a look and in India you do get plenty of chances as it is often the basis of a street show. Unfortunately, our rupees were wasted on this occasion — it soon became apparent that the cobra was safe from any assaults because the usually nimble mongoose had a brick tied to its back leg. I suppose you can't really blame the organiser of the show for this deception, as his act would have been even worse off if he happened to lose one of its stars.

FISH TRAPS
COCHIN, 1998

These contraptions are in fact ingenious devices that are lowered into the water by a pulley system made of vines and bamboo and then lifted again to reveal, hopefully, a successful harvest in the netted area. The reason the traps are all in one line, rather than spread out, is simple — the current runs in and out along a narrow corridor of water, into which the nets dive at precisely the appropriate moment.

MICHAEL SLATER
JAIPUR, 1996

Slats receives the traditional welcome of a garland of flowers around the neck and some facial decoration between the eyes, as we settle into the luxurious Jaipur Palace Hotel before our first-round clash with the West Indies during the 1996 World Cup.

STEVE WAUGH

OUTSIDE THE AMBER FORT, RAJASTHAN, 1996

Appearances can certainly be deceiving and my outwardly-looking calmness was in fact a cover for the tension and anxiety that was running through my body. With a massive, slimy dead weight wrapped around my neck in the form of a python, combined with a cobra in each basket — one on the head and one in the hand — it was no wonder fellow player and in this instance photographer Glenn McGrath kept on adjusting the camera to prolong the agony and give himself a few laughs at my expense. Minutes later, we reversed roles, but being a country boy, Pigeon looked more at home — he wore the snake in much the way he'd wear a gold necklace.

THE GROOM
OLD DELHI, 1998

He looks like a condemned man, but in fact the gentleman cowering under the weight of a garland of flowers atop this spectacularly adorned white horse is a husband-to-be on his way to his wedding ceremony, much to the excitement of the locals looking on.

THE GANGES
CALCUTTA, 1998

While many people in India have few material possessions, personal hygiene is of the utmost importance — these gentlemen are performing their daily ritual with meticulous care.

SURVIVAL OF THE FITTEST
BOMBAY, 1996

With limited facilities available in the lead-up to the '96 World Cup, the Bombay Gymkhana Club came to our rescue providing us with four days of excellent practice wickets. Each day, as we pulled up to the ground and when we departed, a group of street kids would chase us the length of the block in the hope of a few rupee notes going their way. This boy probably earned the most, as he pursued us for the longest distance before we lost him in the swarming traffic.

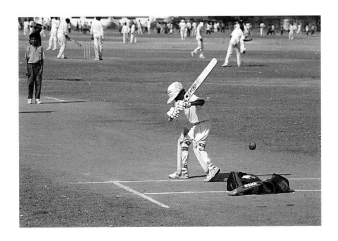

YOUNG CHAMPION
BOMBAY, 1996

This young boy caught my eye during a leisurely lap of the Gymkhana Ground. This myriad of cricket fields, with boundaries overlapping, has been the breeding ground for such greats as Sunil Gavaskar and Sachin Tendulkar. Judging by this youngster's technique and keenness, he's on his way to better things, although when he grows up he'll have to contend with three stumps!

IMAGES OF WAUGH

PENANCE
OLD DELHI, 1998

In India, religion plays a huge part in people's lives, with many going to extraordinary lengths to demonstrate their commitment. Here is just about the ultimate example ...

While sightseeing during a day off on our tour in '98, we came across a scene that even our guide had never encountered before. We heard the sounds of a street parade (opposite, above) and saw the amazing colours that accompanied it, so we edged closer to see what it was all about. And, boy, did we get the shock of our lives.

Soon, right in front of us, stood a group of men (above) eagerly awaiting their turn to have a large skewer speared through their cheeks. No anaesthetic and, more dangerously, no antiseptic to clean the sharp instrument. Not long after, I came across another amazing sight — a young man (opposite, below) who appeared to be almost showing off as he drove a crochet-style needle through his tongue.

Showing only pleasure, no pain, these men seemed on the verge of a trance as they paraded down the street, stopping just briefly for the next in line to take up the challenge and continue the ceremony.

WHISTLIN' BIRDS
CALCUTTA, 1998

Like me, Gavin Robertson is something of a sightseer, so we often head out into the streets to see what the locals are up to and try to get a feel for what the place is all about. Robbo captures it on his video camera, while I take the snapshots on the Canon, and together we are a real pain in the backside for anyone who gets in our way.

The intelligent one in this shot is a street hawker trying to offload his plastic whistlin' birdies, which I'm sure must be harder to sell than the shower curtain rings Del Griffin (aka John Candy) had to flog in 'Planes, Trains and Automobiles'. Perhaps the 'Cheshire cat' smile is the touch needed to keep his business in good shape.

RICKY PONTING
BOMBAY, 1996

It's every outfielder's dream, on a stinking hot day when the game is drifting along aimlessly, to have a pole to prop yourself up against. Protocol certainly doesn't encourage players to lean on fences during international matches, but when it's against a local Bombay XI in a practice game, you'd be silly if you didn't, especially when the scoreboard attendant looks so comfortable only metres away.

Trading Places

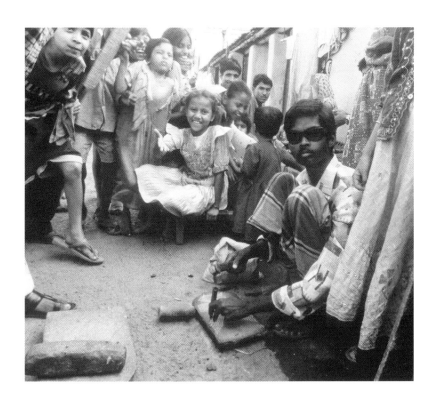

STREET TRADE

CALCUTTA, 1998

If you take a stroll along the thoroughfares and alleyways of any big city in India, you're sure to see a wide variety of street traders, service providers, charlatans and speculators, all hoping to earn at least enough rupees to keep their families fed and under cover. In this chapter are just a few examples — when I see how some of these street-wise artisans have decided to earn a living, I wonder just how they came into such lines of work. Some schemes just don't fit into this bustling kerbside environment and, to me at least, seem destined for failure. But I admire the character and spirit of these people, sometimes marvel at their ingenuity, and hope that they'll all gain enough from their endeavours to keep their humble dreams alive.

On the previous page, a stonemason — complete with Tom Cruise's sunglasses — goes about his business as the kids move in, quick as a flash, desperate to get involved in the photograph, while below is a kerbside diner, just one of many such establishments trying to catch the attention of the multitude rushing by.

BODY MASSAGE
CALCUTTA, 1998

Before entering the Ganges for a wash, you can indulge yourself with a somewhat unconventional massage if you don't mind the odd knee driven into your backbone or the occasional slap around the cranium. Rough as the treatment may appear, the recipient still had enough composure to give the camera a smile of satisfaction, leading me to believe the massage might even be beneficial.

VEGETARIAN'S DELIGHT
CALCUTTA, 1998

I quickly learned that this dish was strictly vegetarian, not long after it was explained to me that the ingredients have to be carefully and continually turned over with the large ladle to make sure that the contents are evenly cooked. The chef was more than happy to let me have a sample, while his fellow workers just wanted to get into the picture frame.

STREET VENDOR
BOMBAY, 1998

Either the guy wasn't happy with his brew, or he didn't want me to discover his secret recipe as I snapped him stirring his concoction on the sidewalk. Mind you, the price of 12 rupees (around 50 cents Australian) seems cheap for such a celebrated product.

CARD SCHOOL
CALCUTTA, 1998

Cards is one of those universal pastimes that brings mates together and, as is the case here, can lead to paranoia about people trying to spy on your hand. The lad giving me the dirty look clearly thought I was offering his opposition some sly signals to bring about his downfall.

HATS AND SPICES
BOMBAY, 1998

The back alleys and side streets of India are full of life and plenty of colour. Combined with the unique smells and unusual sights, they provide a bombardment for all your senses and become scenes that stay forever in your memory.

In this instance, I'm not sure if you receive a free hat with every fruit or spice purchase, but whatever you fancy, the options are plentiful.

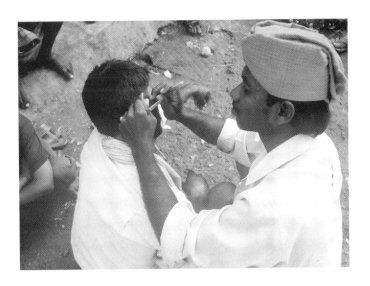

EAR CLEANER
NEW DELHI, 1998

With a population of around one billion people and no social security system available to the unemployed in India, it's up to everyone to eke out a living the best way they can. This is one of the more novel occupations used to pay the bills. At one rupee per inspection, the poor bloke's going to have to find quite a few heads to make ends meet.

COCONUT SELLER
BOMBAY, 1996

I'm not sure how many coconuts this bloke parts with in a typical day, but I know it's sure hard to make a profit when you take a nap on the job during the middle of the afternoon.

STRENGTH AND SKILL

BOMBAY, 1996

The sights in India never cease to amaze me. The strength of many of the workers in the big cities is quite astounding and even more incredible when you take into account the temperatures, density of traffic and the long hours they put in.

These two guys not only have tremendous strength, but also, clearly, a detailed knowledge of how to effectively stack heavy, cumbersome loads so they can successfully meander down the streets of Bombay.

CATCH OF THE DAY
VISAKHAPATNAM, 1996

Being a spectator at the fish markets in 'Vizag', on the Indian east coast, as the fresh hauls are brought onto the dock from the various deep-sea expeditions is enough to turn you into a vegetarian. With no refrigeration and little ice available, the stench is quite repugnant and to try to counteract this problem, sawdust is used to preserve the fish.

Seeing fish scooped up into wheelbarrow-like carts with shovel and shoe is also a bit of an eye-opener, but nothing compared to watching the locals going into battle over the value of their catches once the negotiating begins.

MAN IN THE OVEN
CALCUTTA, 1998

As you walk along an Indian street, there is always something that will catch your eye. As I strolled through this busy thoroughfare I noticed some food preparation taking place, a common enough occurrence, but from out of the oven itself I spotted a pair of eyes and some pearly whites. Upon further inspection, I realised it was indeed the cook getting right among it, preparing his culinary delights in probably the hottest and most cramped conditions anywhere in the world.

FISH MARKETS
CALCUTTA, 1998

Looks like a pretty good day's work, with just this solitary offering remaining in the display area. Hopefully, it didn't make it through to the next day's trading, as we'd noticed a rather large black crow having a bit of a peck at its entrails moments before the crowd started congregating in the background.

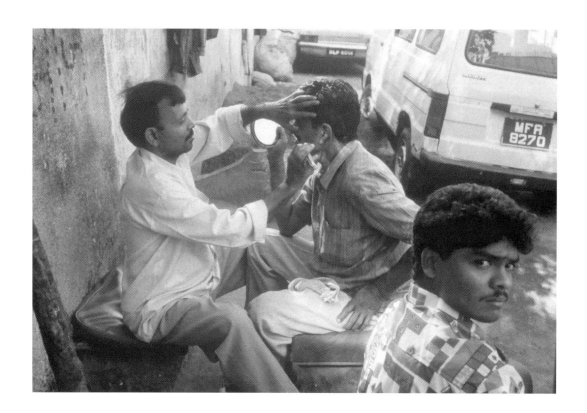

KERBSIDE BARBER
BOMBAY, 1998

It may seem a little primitive to ask for a shave on the way to work, but there are plenty of barbers on the pavement to choose from and by all accounts they offer a pretty close shave.

SWEET SMILE
MADRAS, 1998

This young girl captured my attention every day as we made our trip to the ground for the Madras Test. Even though she quite clearly had very little in the way of material possessions, and even though she was devoting her entire day to selling her sweets from the curb and gutter of a very busy road, she never failed to smile as we made our way back and forth from the hotel.

GRANT ROAD
BOMBAY, 1996

In every major city of the world, the oldest profession has a stranglehold on one part of town. In Bombay, it's the infamous Grant Road. As I always want to see the good and the bad of each place I visit, I asked the taxi driver to show me everything, and that he did.

The scene from my cab window was almost macabre, with transvestites, pimps and prostitutes emerging from their cage-like enclosures to offer their wares, simply in order to survive.

FALSE CHARITY

BOMBAY, 1996

To someone not used to seeing a beggar in action, the experience can have a profound impact. Most probably, you will either feel so desperately sorry for them that you will hand over all your spare rupees or you will be so shocked that you'll turn a blind eye and pretend it's not happening.

The image of a mother holding an undernourished baby is especially disconcerting and disturbing, but doubly so when you know that the whole thing is a form of organised crime.

The truth is that the baby was hired out for the day to the 'mother', who then went out and begged for money that would, at the end of the day, be handed over to the head of the scam — a 'standover type' individual. This person will profit from all of the many such schemes being perpetrated on his turf, leaving the women and children with a meal but very little else to show for their efforts.

Behind the Dressing-room Door

IAN MCDONALD AND PAUL REIFFEL
ADELAIDE, 1998

These boys could sure whistle a good tune if they got together! Macca, our much-loved team manager, regularly sheds his false teeth to perform his favourite number from his repertoire, 'Suzie', after a team win — so his look was no surprise to us all. Pistol's fake dentures, on the other hand, were a pretty well-kept secret, having only come into existence after his front fang hit the turf at Bellerive Oval in Hobart during an Aussie Rules match before a Victoria–Tasmania Sheffield Shield match. A team-mate's elbow had caught him flush in the face.

I reckon Pistol should forget about getting his smile fixed. Instead, he should work on a bit of a snarl in his follow-through. Any batsman would find that intimidating.

In the photograph on page 101, the longest-serving member of the Australian cricket squad, physiotherapist Errol Alcott, who arrived on the scene in 1984, is giving Macca an ice shower in the Adelaide Oval dressing room in early 1997. In the background is Greg Blewett (left) and the 'great one' Nugget Rees, who is guarding the replica of The Frank Worrell Trophy which the lads had gratefully presented to him after our series victory earlier in the day.

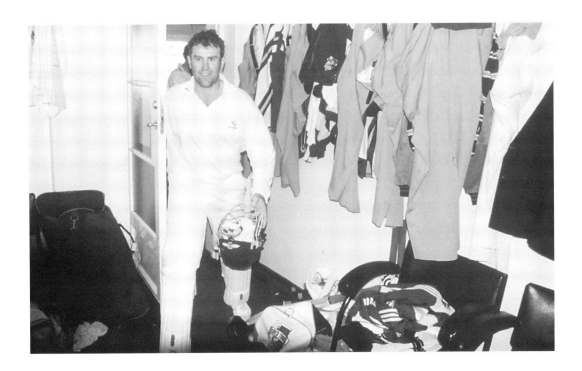

MARK TAYLOR
BIRMINGHAM, 1997

Our captain went into the second innings of the First Test of the '97 Ashes series knowing that a failure here could easily have meant that this would have been his last innings in Test cricket. Thus, these photographs, taken after Mark had scored one of the most courageous Test hundreds you could ever wish to see, capture a significant part of cricket history.

Tubs looks rightfully pleased with himself. The first photograph captures his adrenalin-charged walk into the dressing-room area, where he copped plenty of backslapping and complimentary words. The second is a vastly different image — here is a man, in the comfort of his chair, relieved and contented as he begins to contemplate what he has just achieved.

It's always fantastic to see a team-mate pull through under the most adverse conditions, as it not only makes everyone feel good but also sets an example that anything can be achieved if you really want it and believe you can do it.

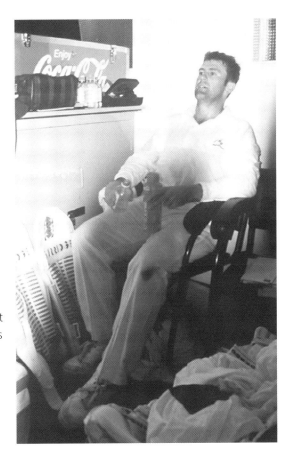

NUGGET REES
ADELAIDE, 1997

Ask anyone who knows Barry Rees and they'll tell you the same thing, 'What a great bloke, he's an absolute legend.'

I've never heard a bad word uttered about the man known to everyone as 'Nugget', a guy who is the most dedicated and loyal supporter of the Adelaide Crows, the South Australian Sheffield Shield team and the Australian cricket team that you'd ever meet.

From a humble beginning dusting tennis racquets at the Rowe and Jarman sports store in Adelaide some 30 odd years ago, Nugget has become as much a part of the Adelaide Oval as the old wooden scoreboard or the majestic cathedrals that encompass this wonderful sporting arena. He is renowned for his humble, kind and gentle nature, and he owns the best set of manners that anyone has ever encountered.

During one-day games and Test matches we consider him part of our team. As players, that is the highest compliment we can give. Mind you, Nugget always gives out more than he gets. He is forever willing to run errands for the good of the team and look out if anyone says anything against one of his players. Nugget is such a parochial supporter that singles are clapped as if someone has just posted three figures, and anything that hits the pads when the opposition goes into bat is always out. Each morning, Nugget arrives about 30 minutes before play, but never walks into the dressing-room area without first knocking on the door, to ask permission to enter. Immaculately dressed, always with a tie, and clean shaven, Nugget lights up the room with enthusiasm and warmth as soon as he arrives.

In recent years, Nugget's thunderous applause for anything good Australia does on the field has led to a need for him to actually wear a pair of batting gloves — to muffle the noise he makes — while he watches every ball as if his life depends upon it.

During my career, Nugget has given many inspirational team talks atop the dressing-room table. On each occasion he has lifted the players to a higher level. Some of his favourite lines are 'keep the throws up to the keeper', 'make sure you're watching the captain', 'plenty of support for the bowlers', and 'plenty of chat in the field'. By the time Nugget has covered every aspect of our game we're ready to take on the world. Nugget, meanwhile, settles down to his favourite seat, in the far corner of the second row.

Playing at Adelaide is a great occasion for all cricketers, but the presence of Nugget in our corner makes it that little bit more special. I for one couldn't imagine being in the dressing-room and not hearing him say 'what goes on tour, stays on tour' and 'thanks very much' at least twice a day.

Nugget's pictured here in the Adelaide Oval dressing-room during the Fourth Test of the 1996–97 series against the West Indies, wearing, as usual, the Australian baggy green cap that the great Norm O'Neill presented to him in 1962.

BEHIND THE DRESSING-ROOM DOOR

105

THE AUSTRALIANS
ADELAIDE, 1997

This is the look of a team well satisfied with its efforts. The post-match discussions are about to begin, signalling an end to the revelry that preceded it.

As you can see, it was pretty hard to wrestle 'Frank' (The Frank Worrell Trophy) from Heals and, as usual, the immortal Nugget Rees is having the time of his life in among the lads.

Warney (left, front) is sitting in his usual dressing-room position for Adelaide. This is a bench full of 'old-timers'. During a day's play, Mark Waugh would be next to him, and on the next two seats, selection and injury permitting, would be myself and Mark Taylor.

BRENDON JULIAN
GEORGETOWN, 1995

Many say BJ will slip straight into 'Melrose Place' or 'Baywatch' when his time is through with the flannels. Here, though, he is celebrating a five-wicket second-innings haul against Guyana during our Caribbean tour of 1995.

FIVE OF A KIND

LONDON, 1997

The Second Test of the '97 Ashes series, at Lord's, was completely ruined by rain. The first day was washed out entirely, and by the end of the scheduled fourth day we had reached just 7–213 (Elliott 112) in our first innings after bowling the Poms out for 77 (McGrath 8–38). Despite the fact that the final day was just about free of interruptions, the match was eventually drawn.

The constant rain meant the lads were obliged to seek any number of ways of passing the time. When we were young we all read about the card-playing antics of the great Doug Walters, but I imagine Australian cricketers were playing cards in the dressing-room during breaks in play long before Dougie first wore the baggy green. Here we see another school in progress, with Glenn McGrath (standing, at left) watching over the strategies of Shane Warne, Michael Bevan, Mark Taylor and Matthew Elliott.

MICHAEL SLATER'S GEAR
ADELAIDE, 1996

Cricket can do funny things to a player's mental state. The game can even get its participants confused about the difference between a kitbag and a toilet bowl.

(Actually, Slats did it to release some pent-up emotion and also to have a bit of a laugh at the situation that had brought about his undoing.)

Keen as he was to build on his memorable 219 against Sri Lanka in Perth in the First Test of the three-match 1995-96 series, Slats probably tried too hard after that innings. He did score 62 in the first innings of the Second Test, in Melbourne, but then failed twice in Adelaide, which led to the scenario captured in this photograph.

Being the last game of the series, Slats thought his gear could do with a bit of a wash, so down the bowl it went, together with some harsh words and a rather tough appraisal of his second-innings dismissal. At first, the boys didn't quite know what all the commotion was about, but once the truth was known, word spread rapidly. Being a compassionate lot, we didn't say anything, didn't let on we knew what happened, while Slats sat among us slowly regaining his composure. But eventually someone had to whisper, 'I don't think the toilet's working any more.'

That broke the ice. As the rest of the lads broke into uncontrollable laughter, Slats knew he'd been found out. The affair ended with the heartiest laughs coming from the bloke whose kitbag was a considerable bit lighter than it had been at the start of the Test.

GAVIN ROBERTSON, ADAM DALE AND DARREN LEHMANN
MADRAS, BANGALORE AND BANGALORE RESPECTIVELY, 1998

On this and the next two pages are the Test debut boys, minutes before they took the field for the first time during their first Test match for Australia.

Robbo looks like a stunned kangaroo on the middle of the Hume Highway, as the approaching Mack truck's high beam becomes brighter and brighter. 'Chippen' Dale was definitely the kid who nervously held the class identification board between his legs for the school photo. But 'Boof' Lehmann is as relaxed as one can get at such a moment, showing the benefits of having been 12th man in a Test match some eight-and-a-bit years before, as well as scoring a truckload of first-class runs before his opportunity finally came.

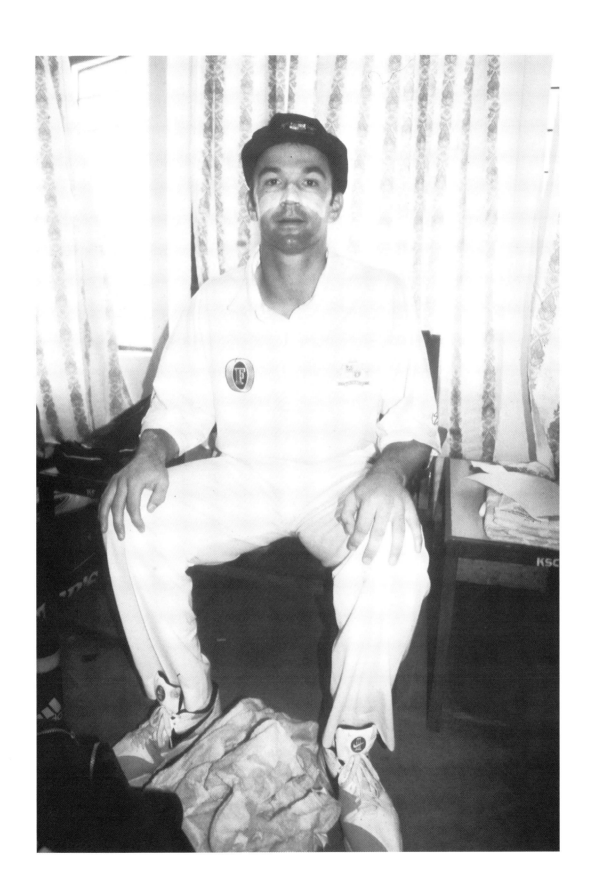

BEHIND THE DRESSING-ROOM DOOR

ALLAN BORDER
DURBAN, 1994

This was the last time AB walked into the Australian team's dressing-room as a player, after batting out the third and final Test of our series in South Africa. The match, and series, ended in a draw.

It was an emotional time for all, because even though our captain refused to say his career was over, we all knew deep down that this was it for one of Australia's greatest-ever players. Our suspicions were basically confirmed very soon after, when he handed out all his gear to the lads. Yours truly snared a prized acquisition — his helmet.

A good trivia question from AB's last innings is: 'Who did he face in his last over of Test cricket?'

The answer: Jonty Rhodes.

WARMING UP

HOVE, 1993

A bit of team bonding after a day's play against Sussex early on the '93 Ashes tour. It was actually a necessity, as the showers weren't working and we'd just come off the ground after fielding all day in bitterly cold and blustery conditions.

This may have been Tim May's first sighting of a camera!

The players in the photograph are (left to right): Maysie, Steve Waugh, Matthew Hayden, Brendon Julian, Damien Martyn, Craig McDermott and Allan Border.

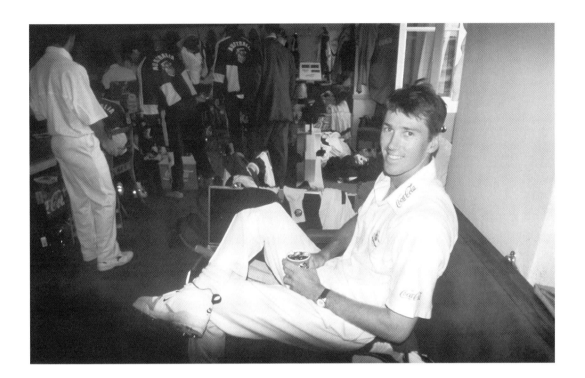

GLENN McGRATH
LONDON, 1997

Pigeon has every right to look satisfied, after demolishing the Poms at Lord's. He captured 8–38 this day and in the process contributed enormously as we bowled England out for just 77.

In fact, Glenn was doubly pleased because of a little side bet he had made with his lounge-seat partner — one SR Waugh.

Cricketers, being a superstitious lot, always head straight to the same seat in a dressing-room that they've occupied when they've previously played there, whether it be in Sydney, Calcutta or Lord's. My piece of dressing-room at Lord's is where this photograph was taken from. It offers me a great view of the centre wicket through a little arched window.

The Test in 1997 was my third at Lord's. As soon as I entered the room, I went straight for my spot. Just after I'd settled, Pigeon pointed at the vacant area at the other end of the lounge and asked, 'Is anyone sitting here, Tug?' With tongue in cheek, I replied, 'No, you can sit there. But only if you take five-for when you bowl.'

Without even blinking, Pigeon shot back, 'No problem, as long as you score 100 as well.' And then he plonked himself down.

Unfortunately, as things turned out I fell exactly 100 short of my obligations. However, the boy from Narromine did our corner proud!

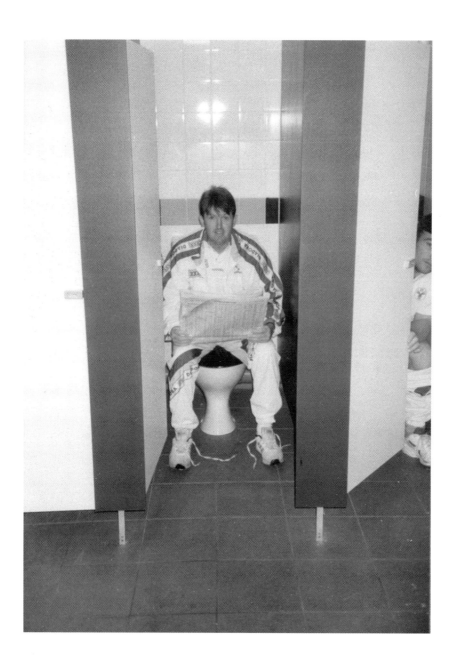

TIM ZOEHRER

LEEDS, 1993

A common problem for all touring teams is the lack of space in dressing-rooms, which are generally designed to cater for 12 players, plus a couple of officials, but no more.

On our '93 Ashes tour, the facilities at Headingley couldn't quite cope with the 17 players and five officials, so Ziggy Zoehrer made himself at home in one of the cubicles for the duration of the Test match. Here he is studying the form, while next door a nervous Michael Slater prepares to do battle for his country.

Matthew Elliott, Greg Blewett and Justin Langer

Nottingham, 1997

The euphoria of our fantastic victory at Trent Bridge, which sealed the fate of the Ashes our way again, obviously got to these three lads — all of whom are actually non-smokers. The drawback that Herbie took is still giving him respiratory problems today, while Blewey's obviously been watching too many Clint Eastwood movies. And Lang? Well, here's a technique that's sure to singe those nose hairs!

STEVE WAUGH, SHANE WARNE AND FRIENDS
SYDNEY, 1998

Can you name these two great long-time supporters of Australian cricket? The keen autograph collector on my right is none other than INXS band member Tim Farris. On Warney's left is John Cornell, the man responsible for making 'Crocodile Dundee' happen but more recognisable to millions of Australians as 'Strop' from the Paul Hogan TV series.

Both gentlemen are loyal and passionate in their following of both forms of cricket and their presence in the dressing-rooms after we toppled South Africa was appreciated by all the lads.

LORD'S DRESSING-ROOM
LONDON, 1997

Times have certainly changed in terms of the way teams prepare for the demands of international cricket and how the players fill in their spare time.

In years gone by, a rain delay in a match would have meant a nice cup of tea and a few biscuits, or maybe a couple of hands of cards. Today it's out with the boxing gloves, the exercise bike, the abdominal roller and some light weights, just to top up those fitness levels. On this occasion, our fitness trainer Steve Smith (sparring with Michael Bevan, while Mark Taylor, hands on hips, looks on) set up a 12-station circuit routine in the confines of the Lord's dressing-room. It seemed his main ambition was to get the boys working off the world-renowned baked dinners and apple pie and ice cream that come so regularly from the kitchens of the MCC.

GLENN MCGRATH, JASON GILLESPIE AND MICHAEL KASPROWICZ

LONDON, 1997

Australia's fast bowling stocks are in great hands with these three guys who, if on the park together, form one of the world's most potent pace attacks. This photograph was taken in The Oval dressing-room after the final Test of the 1997 Ashes series. The good news for Australian cricket is that all three are still improving and have plenty of years ahead of them in the baggy green.

DAVID BOON AND STEVE WAUGH
ADELAIDE, 1996

A final dressing-room farewell to Boonie, who everyone in the Australian team still misses. Boonie's final game was a victory over Sri Lanka, hence the 'soaking wet' look which is always such a pleasure to wear. Nugget Rees is in the background.

IAN HEALY AND RICKY PONTING
CUTTACK, 1996

Punter didn't get his nickname without good reason. As well as having a kennel full of 'dishlickers' winning all over Tasmania, Ricky isn't too bad at the odd hand of blackjack. However, it appears in this photograph that the banker has just rolled him, to snatch away a wad full of rupees during a lengthy rain delay.

You may ask why is Heals the banker. Well, the answer is simple. He was the one smart enough to bring the mobile casino on tour!

MARK TAYLOR

LEEDS, 1997

Tubby punches out his party favourite — Cold Chisel's 'Bow River' — as the boys settle in for the long haul after winning the Fourth Test. However, the festivities were somewhat curtailed when we discovered we had sprayed most of our supply of beer over the floor during our earlier passionate rendition of 'Under the Southern Cross'. Not to be denied, we headed back to the team hotel and celebrated with our families and members of the Canberra Raiders until the early hours.

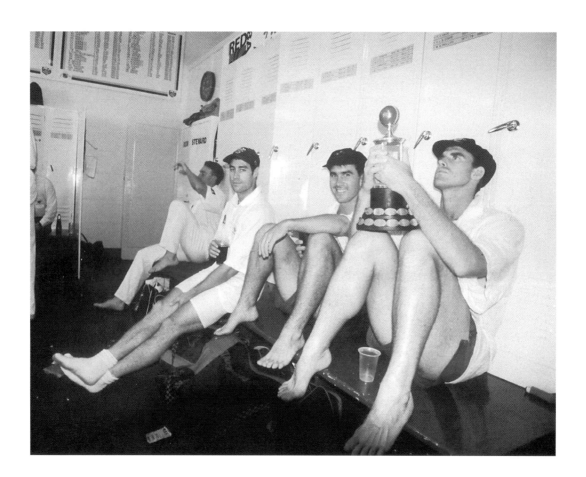

MATTHEW HAYDEN
ADELAIDE, 1997

One can only imagine what's running through Matthew Hayden's mind but, knowing how passionate he is about his cricket, there is no doubt that this was indeed a special moment for him. For Matt, to be part of a winning Test team, in the game that won back for Australia the Frank Worrell Trophy on home soil, and to score your maiden Test-match century in the same match will take some beating.

Making it even more memorable for Matt was the fact that he was playing under enormous pressure, having withstood a torrent of pre-Test media speculation surrounding his selection. To experience the ecstasy of the peaks, you must have already felt the torment of the valleys. His performance in this game proved to me that he is a player who has what it takes to succeed at the top level.

THE AUSTRALIANS
LEEDS, 1997

Headingley has to be one of my favourite venues, not only because I've scored two unbeaten 150s in Test matches there (177 not out in 1989, 157 not out in 1993), but also because there will always be fond memories for me of dressing-room camaraderie and of three decisive Test-match victories (by 210 runs in the First Test of 1989, by an innings and 148 runs in the Fourth Test of 1993, and by an innings and 61 runs in the Fourth Test of 1997).

When we arrived at Leeds in '89 we were told the wicket was a bowler's dream and that it was Australia's 'graveyard' ground — before 1989, Australia had only won five Ashes Tests there, in 19 tries, and none since 1964, and England had won the past three and four of the past five, with the other drawn. But we broke with 'tradition' and totalled over 600 in the first innings of three Headingley Tests in a row.

These walls could tell some amazing tales if they could talk. For now, one very happy picture will have to do.

AROUND THE WORLD

THE WAUGHS AND FRIENDS
TAUNTON, 1997

A special moment on tour — daughter Rosalie's first birthday party, at the Castle Hotel in Taunton, Somerset — celebrated and shared by members of the touring squad and their partners. Rosie seemed to really enjoy everyone's company, which was also important to all the guys. Because we spend so much time together, it means a lot that everyone appreciates sharing moments such as these. During my 13 years playing for Australia I've celebrated only one Christmas and three birthdays at home in Sydney.

For the record, I bought Rosie a Mr Bean doll, which she took back to Australia the day after this birthday.

IAN HEALY AND GLENN MCGRATH
AUCKLAND, 1995

These photographs capture a small but significant part of the way of life of international cricketers in the '90s. Here is the Australian wicketkeeper (left), celebrating his young daughter's birthday in a McDonald's restaurant a long way from their home in Brisbane.

Heals, being the loving, caring father that he is, agreed to have his face painted for the event. And he wasn't the only one to enjoy the party spirit! Little Emma, with her mother's help, had sent out invitations to all the guys in the team and their partners and, reflecting the spirit of the team, even the single lads arrived with presents in hand. Later on, they were seen blowing whistles and wearing party hats, too.

Glenn McGrath opted for the 'incognito' look at the birthday bash. I think he borrowed Adam Gilchrist's ears for the occasion. Or are they Andy Caddick's?

MICHAEL KASPROWICZ
DUBAI, 1998

Kasper showing the skills of a misspent youth, hanging 10 in the Dubai desert while Mark Waugh looks on. Junior, it appears, was not expecting anything too spectacular. And he was right. After an impressive initial leap — as seen here — Kasper gave a wobbly performance down the steep sandslope, ending in an ungainly crash landing with limbs going in all directions. Thankfully, no serious harm was done, as the next day we were required to play in a one-day final against India.

THE FINES COMMITTEE
MADRAS, 1998

The newly-elected Adam Gilchrist, Tom Moody and Damien Fleming ham it up for the camera moments after successfully extracting large amounts of rupees from the wallets of the boys. Just to make themselves feel at ease in unfamiliar surroundings, the trio had proudly donned these makeshift turbans to add a touch of authenticity to the evening.

THE AUSTRALIANS
BERMUDA, 1995

On the way home from our wildly successful tour of the West Indies, the squad stopped off in Bermuda for a series of limited-overs games and a couple of hair-raising days racing around this fantasy island on hired mopeds.

Of course, there were many crashes and mishaps, with perhaps the most memorable belonging to Mark Waugh's fiance, Sue Porter. During the obligatory driver's test, which demanded an incident-free lap of the carpark, Sue managed to confuse the brake and the accelerator. The result was a left-hand turn that went horribly wrong. A parked car might have been narrowly avoided, but a neatly manicured hedge wasn't, and soon after a red-faced driver was scrambling from the wreckage. It was at this point that physio Errol Alcott came up with one of the quotes of the tour. He quietly turned to the local supervisor and asked:

'So, did she pass?'

IAN HEALY AND GLENN MCGRATH

SHANE WARNE AND DAMIEN FLEMING

LAHORE, 1994

On every Australian cricket tour of Pakistan it has become custom for the Australian team to play a doubles tennis tournament on the impressive lawn courts of Lahore. To make the 1994 competition more memorable, it was decided that the pairings (which were determined by a draw out of the hat) would be united not only as a unit but would also be required to dress to match a given theme.

Here we have two of the teams. To the left is the combination of Healy and McGrath, taking us back to the 1930s and the days of Jack Crawford and Adrian Quist. I especially love the belts. And to the right is the duo of Warney and Flemo, who have done well with limited resources. The ties are a nice touch, and though their appearance wasn't enough to intimidate their opponents, they did manage to turn a few heads.

EDEN GARDENS
CALCUTTA, 1998

A bird's eye view of one of the world's most imposing stadiums. The scene was fabulous, but the safety factor wasn't — there was no railing or barrier in front of me when I snapped this photograph.

MICHAEL SLATER
BRANDS HATCH, 1997

In the pits, waiting for a chance to lay down some rubber, is the Australian cricket team's daredevil. Any other drivers out on the track gave Slats a very clear passage once he got on the circuit.

FULL HOUSE
COCHIN, 1998

Not only do the light towers look distorted, most things this day appeared to be out of focus. This was due to the overwhelming heat (upwards of 48°C) and stifling humidity (at least 95 per cent) that engulfed the stadium. The conditions were so oppressive that even quite a few of the Indians suffered sunstroke and heat exhaustion, while our guys, some of whom had just arrived from Australia's much milder temperatures, did it very hard.

While 85,000 people endured the heat to watch the game, Damien Martyn spent most of our innings hovering over the toilet seat, until he was called upon to bat, while Michael Kasprowicz literally couldn't breathe at times during his bowling spells. But to Kasper's credit, he continued on until he looked likely to go from being a casualty to a fatality.

This was the first one-day international to be played in Cochin, which became the 30th city to host a one-dayer in India. The match was eventually won by the locals, to the absolute delight of the sunburnt masses, by 41 runs, 5–309 off 50 overs (Tendulkar 8; Kasprowicz, 8.2 overs, 3–50) to 268 off 45.5 overs (Martyn 4, Tendulkar 5–32). We always knew the little Indian champion was going to be our No. 1 danger, but we thought if he was going to beat us it would have been with his bat!

MARK TAYLOR
TAUNTON, 1993
and
BOB SIMPSON
AUCKLAND, 1993

Despite the best efforts of Tim May and myself, we couldn't find anything worse than the original Daktari for the 1993 Ashes tour, so the reputation this appalling gear had been earning since 1991 continued to grow throughout 1993. How appalling was it? Here are two snapshots of the dreaded 'clothing', being modelled by Tubby Taylor in England in May and by coach Bob Simpson a few weeks earlier in New Zealand.

In fact, Simmo made a complete mockery of the award. The recipient is supposed to despise the outfit, look ridiculous and cringe every time he gets a sideways glance. But here we had the coach looking nice and relaxed and even asking whether he'd be allowed to slide the outfit into his suitcase for the flight back to Australia.

Tubs, as you can see, snared not only the Daktari but also the batsman's curse of the '93 Ashes tour — 'Plucka the Duck'. This little, cute, cuddly toy was the nemesis of all who wielded the willow, with the last man to score nought having the dubious distinction of owning it until a new owner was found.

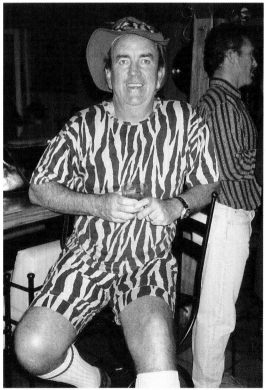

THE CANBERRA RAIDERS
LEEDS, 1997

When you're playing away from home, it's always great to have some Australian support in the crowd. The Aussie flag and voice are distinctive features that don't go unnoticed by the players. Twenty professional rugby league players in ridiculously loud coloured wigs certainly made themselves known to everyone at Headingley during our victorious fifth day of the Fourth Test of the '97 Ashes campaign. To reward the Raiders for their efforts during the day, we invited them into the changerooms for a celebratory ale or two. Our offer was eagerly accepted, and it wasn't long before the boys, still resplendent in their multi-coloured hairdos, were nice and relaxed in their new environment.

Big Mal Meninga was particularly striking in a bright blue wig, while Ricky Stuart's green and Laurie Daley's blue (opposite, above, with Greg Blewett and Matthew Elliott) made them easy targets for the rugby league fans in our squad, including Mark Waugh (opposite, below) who were keen to catch up for a few anecdotes. It developed into a memorable night, with plenty of backslapping and match post-mortems, all washed down with enough 'attitude adjusters' to make everyone wish time could stand still.

Perhaps the only individual who didn't agree with this line of thought was Michael Bevan, who almost came to grief at the hands of Canberra's 'Green Machine'. At one point, Bevo was picked up like a rag doll and tossed triumphantly into the air by a couple of muscle-bound invitees, much to the mirth of all around. Unfortunately for Bevo, the 'tossers' had underestimated their own strength and our male equivalent of Elle Macpherson was projected straight through the roof partitioning, leaving only the lower half of his body visible to those below. A gasp of horror was quickly followed by a symphony of laughter once Bevo's undamaged head came back into view.

As you can see, this incident didn't slow down proceedings. It will be interesting to discover whether the roof has been repaired by the time we return to Headingley in 2001.

JP GETTY'S PRIVATE CRICKET GROUND
IBSTONE, 1997

This is the view from the thatched wooden-cottage dressing-rooms of the mega-rich recluse John Paul Getty's private cricket ground. Guests at the match included Rolling Stone Mick Jagger and fellow musician Marianne Faithfull, who seemed to enjoy the carnival atmosphere; there was a brass band playing and free ice-cream available from 'vendors' roaming the lush grounds.

A highlight for many of us was getting to see Mr Getty's private library, which is valued at over £30 million and includes works such as the first atlas of the world, scrolls from the 12th century and a Bible that belonged to Anne Boleyn, who was the second wife of Henry VIII until she was accused of adultery and executed in 1536.

CROWD CRUSH
GUJRANWALA, 1994

One of the most frightening things I've seen during my career came during this crowd stampede. It occurred at the Jinnah Stadium, a venue in Pakistan that we describe as 'up country' — in other words, it's not located in a major city. For such a place in Pakistan to host an international cricket match, in this case a one-day international between Pakistan and Australia, is a very, very big event indeed for the town's citizens. Many locals are so poor that they had to save a year's wages just to be able to get into the ground.

Sadly, there were two major problems. One, the covers that were supposed to protect the wicket had holes in them, which meant that the pitch had become saturated after overnight rain. And two, 20,000 genuine match tickets had been sold in tandem with an estimated 20,000 counterfeit versions that had been traded through the local black market.

Trying to get 40,000 passionate people into a ground that holds half that number was always going to create a massive problem, but when the fans discovered that no play was likely and no refunds were going to be made the result was a stampede, and then panic. Amid the mayhem hundreds of people were crushed, and then a steel security fence crumpled under the weight.

The sounds of screaming and atmosphere of sheer desperation were horrific, and in the end a major catastrophe was only just avoided as the crowd finally and reluctantly retreated under the pressure of a lathi charge from the local constabulary.

I was the only person who took a photograph of the chaos, and it made the front page of some Australian papers the next day. For me, the most amazing feature of the photograph is the smiling gentleman towards the bottom right-hand corner. At first, he seemed to be in a lot of trouble, but when he saw me he immediately snapped out of his distress and yelled, 'Steve Waugh, you are my most favourite cricketer!' Then he smiled for the camera. And then he returned to his anguish.

Once it was clear a tragedy had been averted, the local police commissioner approached our management and said, 'We must have a game or else none of us will get out of here alive!'

It's amazing what a few words of encouragement can do to get things moving. While it was impossible to play a fair dinkum game, we put on a carnival-type limited-overs match that appeased the locals sufficiently and we were able to safely exit Gujranwala at day's end.

STEVE WAUGH, MERV HUGHES, DEAN JONES AND GEOFF LAWSON
NIAGARA FALLS, 1989

Do we look like tourists? The four of us were among a group who experienced the Falls before a World XI v West Indies exhibition match at the indoor Skydome in Toronto in early November 1989.

Incidentally, a crowd of 35,000 came along to watch the game, which was played on Astroturf and was won, not surprisingly, by our opponents. The Windies quicks quite enjoyed the extra bounce they were able to generate from a lively-paced surface.

AN AUSTRALIAN CAMEL TRAIN
DUBAI, 1998

Enjoying the hospitality of the locals and one of their traditional modes of transport on the sands just outside Sharjah in the Middle East. This activity was part of an enjoyable day relaxing away from the cricket field. Such recreation while on tour is becoming more and more vital because of the increasingly congested schedules given to today's top players.

GLENN McGRATH
DURBAN, 1994

The team's social committee introduced a new bonding exercise during our tour of '94, which required each of the players to go out and buy the worst shirt possible, complete with an accessory if so desired, for a designated colleague. Whom you purchased for was determined by a draw out of a hat.

In the event, some quite horrendous numbers were handed over. Justin Langer was seen modelling a see-through lace top, while S. Waugh looked a little vulnerable in a brightly-coloured halter top. However, fortunately (for me), Glenn won the Daktari award and in recognition of his 'achievement' was forced to wear his atrocious gift to a 'well-to-do' nightclub in Durban, much to the delight of the lads. His attire certainly proved a topical conversation point for all at the club until, almost mercifully, midnight came around and our paceman's torture was complete.

JUSTIN LANGER
SUN CITY, 1997

Lang loves being in a photo more than Bruce Willis and Demi Moore. Here he is lounging around at this world-famous tourist resort during a two-day break on our successful tour of South Africa.

BETWEEN THE LINES
MULTAN, 1994

As I was strolling down a lane in one of the most ancient cities in the world during our tour of Pakistan in 1994, I came across the image of this man who, with his relaxed gaze out over the myriad of electrical wires, seemed to perfectly capture the mood of the place.

LORD'S
LONDON, 1997

A sad sight for everyone, a washout at the home of cricket. It is a dream for every Aussie player to set foot on the hallowed turf, and for each Aussie supporter the enjoyment of watching a game at this great venue is equally stimulating. The whole place has an aura which symbolises its greatness — from the massive slope of the playing surface to the archaic rule of having only men allowed in the famous Long Room, where the immortal WG Grace oil canvas hangs.

It was another strange little quirk that caught me out the first time I ever played there, back in 1988, for Somerset against Middlesex in a one-day game. Each incoming batsman has to walk from the dressing-room, down two flights of stairs, through a doorway, then along the Long Room and through another set of doors before detouring out onto the playing surface. On this occasion, being somewhat nervous and emotional, as soon as I entered the Long Room and saw a room full of elderly gents in their 'egg and bacon' (yellow and brown striped) ties, puffing on their cigars, I panicked and thought I'd come the wrong way. So I scurried for the nearest exit, only to emerge onto the ground some 25 metres from where I was supposed to be. You reckon the local Middlesex boys and my team-mates didn't enjoy seeing a young Aussie suffer such a nightmare?

ERROL ALCOTT

COLOMBO, 1994

The Sri Lankan Daktari, modelled by our long-time physiotherapist. It must be said that Errol was hurting badly when this photograph was taken. He's a man renowned for his classy, cool appearance.

IT'S A HARD LIFE

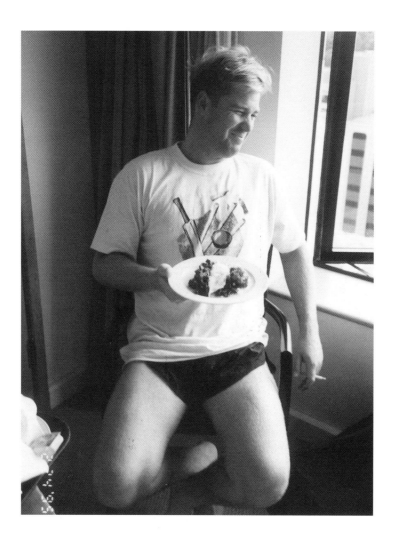

SHANE WARNE
AUCKLAND, 1995

I had to beg Warney for this photograph. Anyone who knows Shane will be stunned to see him even remotely close to a mushroom — such is the genius' disgust for the fungi.

Of course, I was fully aware of this when I noticed he had foolishly put his room service breakfast order on the outside doorknob before the rest of the team had bedded down for the night. Shane's diet is at best pretty basic, so the offerings on the menu presented me with plenty of scope to encourage him to broaden his horizons.

Upon opening his door the following morning, Warney was surprised by the pile of silver trays in front of him and then alarmed when he began removing the lids. Staring straight at him were bowls of porridge, a plate of fresh prunes, grapefruit juice (two glasses), a neat serving of kippers on toast and a mushroom omelette (extra mushrooms, please!).

Warney told me later that he almost heaved on the spot, and that days later he could still smell the mushrooms' ugly aroma.

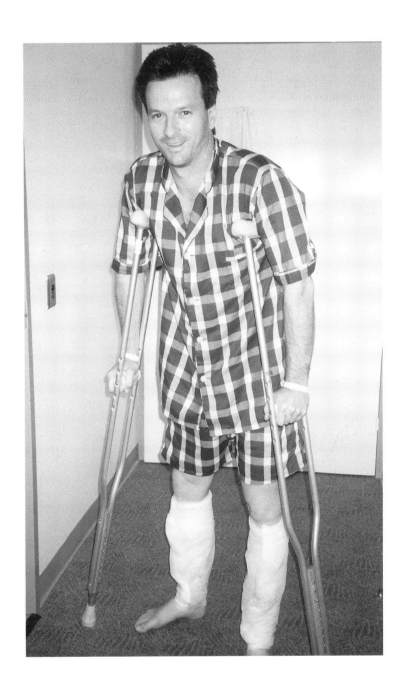

STEVE WAUGH

MELBOURNE, 1996

This photograph was taken while I was recovering from an Anterior Compartment Syndrome fasciotomy to both legs during a rare break in our playing schedule during the Australian winter of 1996. It was two weeks before I was able to get around without the crutches.

While I went in primarily to fix up my lower legs, I also took the chance to have an obdurate nerve decompression release performed on my right groin.

MARK TAYLOR
BIRMINGHAM, 1989

Tubby in the Edgbaston dressing-rooms, having just felt the wrath of coach Bob Simpson's blade during a fielding drill on the '89 Ashes tour. Even Tub's cat-like reflexes weren't enough to repel a sharply-hit slip catch.

To sharpen us up, our fielding practice is always designed to be as close to game-like in intensity as possible. This approach can occasionally lead to an injury to a player ...

And another 'trophy' for Simmo!

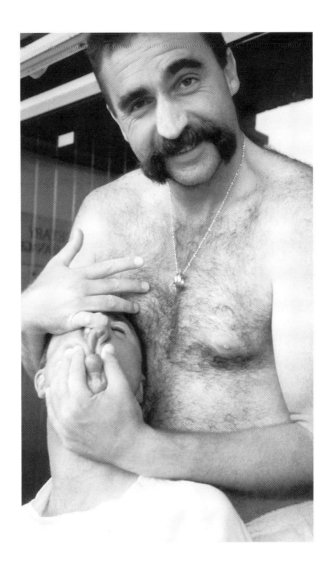

MERV HUGHES AND TIM MAY
ESSEX, 1993

Diligent as ever, Big Merv — perhaps with an eye to a future career with the World Wrestling Federation — applies a nasty facial reconstruction on his always helpless but highly popular team-mate.

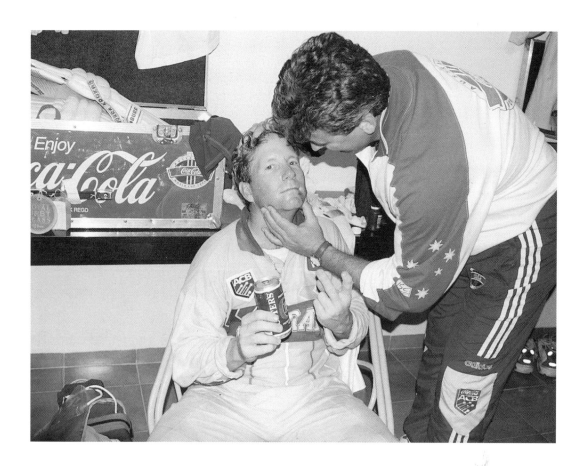

IAN HEALY
CHANDIGARH, 1996

I'm surprised Heals is giving me the two-fingered peace sign rather than the one-fingered 'bird'. The reason Errol Alcott is checking him out for a possible broken jaw and attending to a nasty gash is because of an atrocious throw that came from the photographer. During a botched attempted run-out, my inaccurate throw landed in the bowlers' footholes and leapt awkwardly into Heals' melon before his gloves could intercept the danger.

This incident, however, was only a minor hiccup in one of our greatest, if not our greatest, one-day international wins. In the 1996 World Cup semi-final, the West Indies needed 43 to win with eight wickets in hand and 8.5 overs remaining, but still lost by five runs in the final over, as we produced one of the most remarkable and courageous comebacks in the history of the one-day game. Even the Windies were impressed with our victory, so much so that the normally silent voice of the great Curtly Ambrose remarked, 'Well played. Don't wast' it now, mon. Go all the way.'

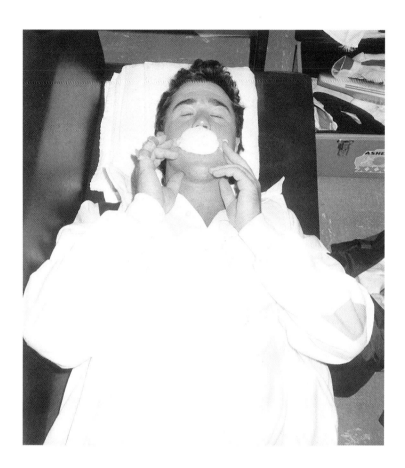

TIM MAY

LONDON, 1989

In the late 1980s, following the departure from the Australian side of Greg Ritchie, Tim May took over as Australia's 'Master of Disaster'. If something strange, unfortunate or downright wacky was to happen, you could bet good money Maysie would feature prominently.

This mishap occurred during our traditional two-day warm-up at Lord's, shortly after arriving in England for another rigorous four-month Ashes campaign. Typically for Tim, this was a freak accident. Big Tom Moody, who strikes the ball as hard as anyone in the game, was flexing his muscles in the nets — clean-hitting some towering 'sixes' and also firing some 'scud missiles' that travelled a long, long way before landing without ever getting more than a metre or two above the turf.

It was one of the scuds that locked onto poor Maysie, who was a good 80 metres away doing some touch-toeing, in an effort to get his rusty body into gear. Someone shouted, 'Look out, Maysie!!' At just the moment Maysie looked up to see what all the fuss was about, the five and a half ounces of hurtling leather skimmed off the greasy surface and hurtled straight into a dumbstruck Tim May.

He hit the deck like a mortally wounded animal. But once it was established that our off-spinner would live to fight another day, the story became a favourite, to be recalled time and again whenever a laugh or two was needed by the lads.

STEVE WAUGH AND STEVE SMITH
LONDON, 1997

Greg Blewett (right) obviously doesn't think much of my chances of winning the world heavyweight crown as he watches me go through my paces at a boxing session with Smithy, our fitness trainer, during a rain delay in the Lord's Test.

The character in the background you can see labouring through a series of sit-ups is our coach, Geoff Marsh.

DARREN BERRY
BRANDS HATCH, 1997

One of the highlights of the '97 Ashes tour was spending a day at former Formula-One world champion Nigel Mansell's driving school, learning how to drive at high speeds. After a 15-minute tutorial, we attacked the circuit in BMWs, with an instructor in the passenger seat to ensure we stayed pretty much on track. Then our adventure moved to a three-lap excursion in a Formula-Three car, with speeds reaching upwards of 90 miles per hour.

To cap the day off, we had the option of being in the passenger seat next to Mark Webber, an Australian hoping to graduate to Formula One in the near future, for a two-lap dash at race speeds. As you can see, it took a bit of convincing to get 'Chuck' Berry into the car. And I can assure you his complexion faded even more noticeably as each returning passenger recounted their thoughts of horror as they had torn into that first sharp right-hand corner of the track.

RICKY PONTING AND ADAM DALE
ABOVE NEW DELHI, 1998

Team-mates always show plenty of compassion for each other, especially if someone is on the verge of throwing up on a plane. The doomed one on this occasion is Adam Dale, who had been ill all week with a stomach virus that would eventually see him lose a total of five kilos and much of his strength. Punter was ready to come to his rescue this time.

As Adam was spurred on by calls of 'Do you want an anchovy thickshake?' and 'How about some nice greasy bacon and eggs?' it was nothing short of a miracle that the sickness bag remained unused.

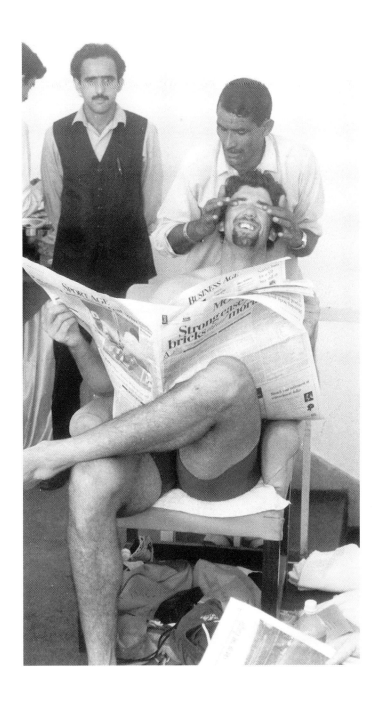

JO ANGEL
RAWALPINDI, 1994

Big Jo was just trying to relax during the lunch break in the Test at Rawalpindi during the 1994 tour. However, the masseur, whom we'd nicknamed 'Fingers', was, in one word, 'enthusiastic', as he attended to every part of the body he reckoned might need some attention. By the time he reached Jo's eyeballs, we felt he was beginning to overstep his welcome.

GLENN MCGRATH
COLOMBO, 1996

The more danger the better for Glenn McGrath. Here is a man who spends his time waiting for a steak in a restaurant by playing Russian Roulette with a knife and the fingers of one hand spread out like a starfish. The idea is to close your eyes and then jab, quick as you can, with the knife at the gaps between the digits. If you play well, you don't lose a finger.

Knowing this is Pigeon's approach to life makes it easier to understand why, when we arrived at our hotel, he allowed this welcoming elephant to latch onto his upper body and lift him clean off the ground. Later in the afternoon, Pigeon admitted that during the escapade he could feel his shoulder beginning to pop out under the weight of the jumbo, which no doubt would have pleased team management immensely, given that we had an international game the next day!

STEVE WAUGH
VERWOERDBURG, 1997

I'm not sure who's given me the most ice-packs during my career — Allan Donald or Curtly Ambrose. But on this occasion it was Donald doing the damage, during the third and final Test of our series in 1997, at Centurion Park. Being 2–0 down, the South Africans were playing not only for their Test careers, but also for their pride, so it was no surprise that they came out breathing fire.

All three of my knocks that required ice eventuated during probably the fastest, nastiest over that I've ever faced in international cricket. Four of Donald's six balls crashed into my body — two into the fingers, one to the ribs, the other to the groin. The fifth delivery whistled past the grill of my helmet and the sixth beat the outside edge.

This might all seem pretty terrifying, but in fact it was one of the most challenging and enjoyable overs of my career. It presented me with one of those periods of sport that test you to the limit. It's what Test-match cricket is all about.

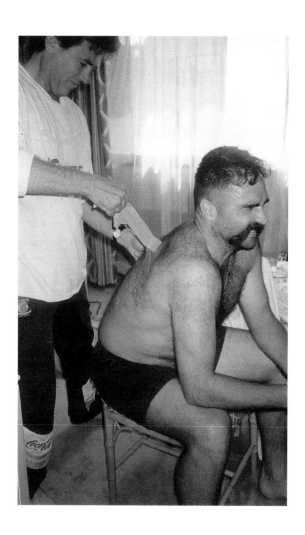

MERV HUGHES
JOHANNESBURG, 1994

Unfortunately for Merv, the long and arduous plane trip to South Africa led to painful back spasms during the opening days of our tour. To help alleviate the discomfort and mend the ailment, Errol Alcott strapped some very powerful and very sticky tape to Merv's back to improve his posture and 'settle' the whole area down. Our physio's prognosis was that this technique would do the trick, which was good news for Merv and for the rest of the team, too, as we needed him back on deck as soon as possible.

An added bonus for us all was a big minus for our strike bowler. The tape had to eventually come off, which was not a pretty prospect for a bloke who doesn't need his back shaved — he needs it lawn-mowed!

Inevitably, a huge crowd gathered when word got out that the operation was about to take place. As things turned out, the event almost turned into an entire evening's entertainment, such was the mammoth size of the task. Mind you, our riotous laughter definitely encouraged Errol to make the process as slow and painful as possible.

GREG BLEWETT

LONDON, 1997

While the rain continued to tumble down outside the Lord's dressing-room, Blewey took it very, very easy inside. Perhaps he was dreaming about getting his name up on the honour board above his head, which recognises anyone who scores a Test century on the hallowed turf?

A Bit of Shut-eye
New Delhi, 1996

Here is an international cricketer's favourite place for catching up on any lost sleep — the airport waiting lounge. The boys have certainly made themselves comfortable here, which was a good idea because the flight was delayed for two-and-a-half hours. The man with the premier position, stretched out luxuriously on the lounge, is the extremely popular Pete McIntyre, a man of immense value to any team — not only for his cricket ability but also for his sense of humour.

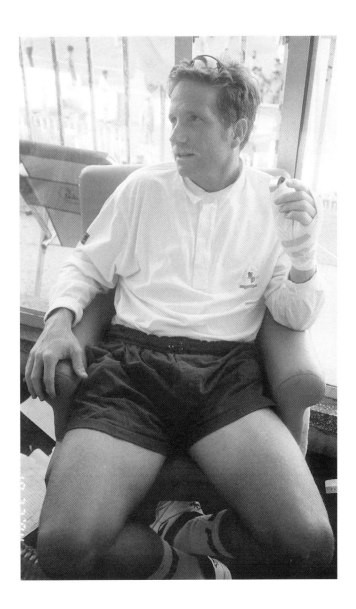

IAN HEALY
RAWALPINDI, 1994

There are two unique features to this photograph. One is obvious, but the other will test your eyesight. The stand-out is the heavily-splinted broken finger which forced Heals to miss a Test for the only time in his long international career. The other feature revolves around the light, shadowy image above Heals' top lip. Try as he might, this was the best he could manage in the team's facial growth contest, which ran over a four-week period.

This was embarrassing for Heals, but for the rest of the lads the 'moustache' provided a great deal of humour, which is essential on a tour as tough and demanding as is Pakistan. Luckily for Heals, we didn't encounter any strong winds or cross the paths of any thirsty cats, or else it might easily have perished long before it reached full 'maturity'.

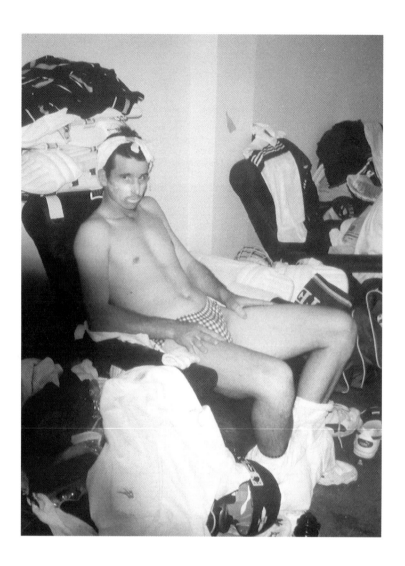

GAVIN ROBERTSON
CALCUTTA, 1998

The human equivalent of a car running out of petrol ...

Robbo was absolutely wasted at the end of the second day's play of the Second Test of the '98 series in India, as the locals and in particular Mohammad Azharuddin and Sachin Tendulkar drove home their strong position. To be fair to Gavin, it must be remembered the temperature was well over the 100 mark on the old scale (more than 38°C), he'd bowled with a fever and had been selected for Australia 'out of the blue' after playing just four first-class games in the previous three years. Bowling off-breaks and fielding in these conditions was as hard a way to get match fit as you could possibly imagine, but to his credit he ended up as our most successful bowler in the Test series, taking 12 wickets.

On the downside was his choice of underwear: as he'd broken the golden rule — don't wear checked colours or lines under white cricket pants.

THE AUSTRALIANS
LONDON, 1997

It's pretty easy to spot the difference between a winning dressing-room and a losing one. Many people said this Test, the sixth and final game of the 1997 Ashes series, at The Oval, was a dead rubber because the fate of the tiny urn had already been decided. However, as you can see this certainly wasn't the feeling of the Aussie players immediately after the match had been decided. Losing this Test meant the series scoreline finished 3–2 instead of 4–1, which was a huge disappointment considering we only needed 124 in the last innings to win the game.

FOR RICHER OR POORER

WHITE TIGER
CALCUTTA, 1998

This gravely-endangered white tiger has sized me up through the bars of the over 100-year-old Calcutta Zoo. Visiting a zoo is a favourite pastime of mine, particularly before a Test match. I find it very relaxing, although after seeing the lack of weight on the 40 or so big cats in Calcutta I was left feeling a bit uneasy. Life is tough for all in the City of Joy.

WASHING SHEDS

BOMBAY, 1996

One of the more popular tourist stops in Bombay is the well-known washing sheds, where the locals can use the facilities for a small fee.

Looking down from the roadside pavement, one is bombarded with a kaleidoscope of colour, and of bodies, together with a chorus of slapping noises as the cloth materials are beaten to a near pulp in the quest for a clean product.

NEAR THE TAJ HOTEL
BOMBAY, 1998

Some people may find this image a little shocking, but to many of India's poor such actions are a necessity as 'luxuries' such as sewerage, electricity and fresh water are not available to them. Early morning is a time for contemplation and these three guys seem to be on the same wavelength.

Perhaps the greatest tragedy of this photograph is that it was taken within walking distance of one of Bombay's finest and most glamorous hotels.

TITANIC
BOMBAY, 1998

The Hollywood blockbuster had no trouble finding its way to India and proved a smash hit — tickets were harder to find for the movie in Bombay than for the ship that ran into the iceberg.

VILLAGE LIFE
COLOMBO, 1996

I found time to take this photograph of some locals, just outside of Colombo, on the day I filed my first story as a TV presenter. Even these people, who have so very few material possessions, are influenced by the marketeers, the power of television and, especially, the power of sport. The young boy on the far left is proudly sporting a Chicago Bears NFL t-shirt, even though to most Sri Lankans a gridiron is probably something that helps press your pants.

BEGGING ON THE STREET
BOMBAY, 1996

Life can be tough on the streets of India for just about anyone, but having a physical disability must make it so disheartening and cruelly difficult. Sadly, begging to have passersby toss money into this metal bucket is the only way this woman can survive. Here she is perched on the steps of the inevitably-crowded thoroughfare to the washing sheds of Bombay.

THE AUSTRALIANS
AGRA, 1996

If you ever want to bring attention to yourself or would like to try to stand out in a crowd, I suggest you wear a yellow Australian one-day outfit, complete with your name on the back, and then walk around one of the seven man-made wonders of the world flanked by security forces armed with sub-machine guns.

The idea of a team photo at the Taj Mahal sounded like a great idea in theory and the end product became a marvellous keepsake for the boys. However, its production certainly created a fair amount of excitement and chaos once the locals took a couple of seconds to work out that an international cricket team was in their midst.

The guys in the team photo on page 167 are:

Back row (left to right): Ian McDonald (media manager), Michael Slater, Damien Fleming, Shane Lee, Glenn McGrath, Jason Gillespie, Paul Reiffel, Stuart Law, Ricky Ponting, Mike Walsh (scorer). Front row: Shane Warne, Steve Waugh, Mark Taylor, Col Egar (manager), Ian Healy, Mark Waugh, Bob Simpson (coach).

MICHAEL SLATER AND COMPANY
NEW DELHI, 1996

Always eager to please, our Indian hosts put on a cultural show for our benefit and during the festivities invited the Indian side, who were also in attendance, to perform an impromptu act. But our opponents declined the invitation.

Looking to seize an early psychological advantage, Slats put his hand up for Australia and did his thing on the dance floor. Then, feeding off his energy, the entire Australian team graced the stage and belted out our favourite Cold Chisel classic, 'Khe Sanh', much to the delight of an audience who were also clearly in shock at our ill-found confidence.

I must stress that this was a totally alcohol-free performance!

DRINKS BREAK
BOMBAY, 1996

There's one thing certain about our hosts at the exclusive Bombay Gymkhana Club — they were extremely anxious to impress. During this practice match before the '96 World Cup they pulled the drinks waiters straight out of the clubhouse bar facilities to serve refreshments on trays to the Australian team on the field. I can tell you we needed them in the oppressive conditions.

IAN HEALY
NEW DELHI, 1996

Our on-field performances during our winless tour of India certainly weren't anything to smile about, but being in New Delhi for the opening day of the first McDonald's on the sub-continent was! However, all wasn't the same once we checked out the menu, with no beef burgers available because the cow is sacred in India. In its place stood the Maharaja Burger, a lamb pattie that on first taste wasn't going to win over the masses. But by a couple of days down the track it was beginning to command some respect, unlike the vegetarian McNuggets, which got a big thumbs down from all who tried them.

MICHAEL SLATER AND PETER MCINTYRE
NEW DELHI, 1996

Instead of the usual team photograph, in front of a pavilion or in the gardens of the team hotel, our management 'sniffed' out this location to give the moment a more historic feel.

The backdrop to this impressive photograph is a monument erected to honour Mahatma Gandhi's famous 380-kilometre, 22-day trek from Sabarmati Ashram, near Ahmedabad, to the sea at Dandi, on the Indian west coast. This was the 'salt march', an epic protest against British rule and specifically their salt monopoly and the crippling taxes on the purchase of this basic commodity that worked so unfairly against the poor. Gandhi set out on the march to bring world attention to his people's plight, a 'battle of Right against Might' was how he described it.

Sixty-six years later, Slats and Aussie Mac joined the gathering, with our opener looking to draw some inspiration from the memory of one of the greatest leaders of the 20th century.

THE AUSTRALIANS
NEW DELHI, 1996

Back row (left to right): Errol Alcott (physio), Stuart Law, Paul Reiffel, Glenn McGrath, Jason Gillespie, Adam Gilchrist, Damien Fleming, Peter McIntyre, Brad Hogg. Front row: Ricky Ponting, Michael Bevan, Geoff Marsh (coach), Mark Taylor, Cam Battersby (manager), Ian Healy, Mark Waugh, Steve Waugh, Michael Slater.

GARDEN PARTY
JAIPUR, 1996

A relaxing day out at the invitation of the Maharajah of Jaipur was a pleasant break from the intensity of our preparations before our impending game against the West Indies. The musical instrument is a local piece of inventiveness and certainly creates an unusual sound that is very relaxing. Slats, as keen as ever to broaden his musical horizons, tried his hand at the harmonica, which mustn't have been too impressive because no-one is taking any notice of his skills.

The Aussies in the photo are (left to right): Ian Healy (sitting on the grass), Michael Slater, Damien Fleming, Shane Lee and Ricky Ponting.

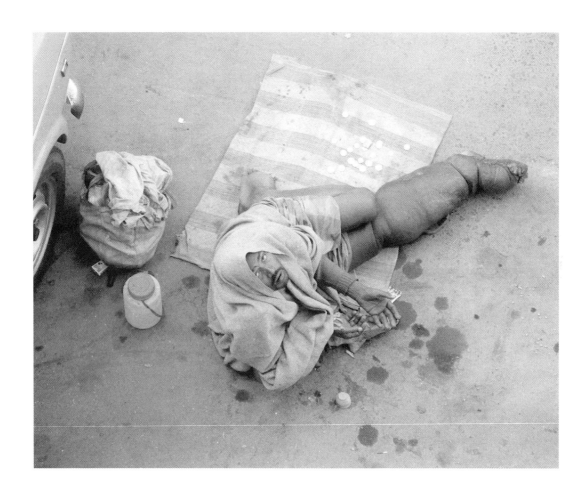

STREET SCENE
CALCUTTA, 1996

This is one of the most brutal and disturbing images that I've seen in 12 years of touring as an Australian cricketer. It was the very first day of our World Cup tour. Shortly after Glenn McGrath and I had acquainted ourselves with the hotel room and decided upon who would have which bed, we agreed that the room was in desperate need of some fresh air. But when we opened the window, we came across the tragic sight, three floors below, of a man grotesquely deformed from the waist down. He was begging for money, caught in a helpless pose that still upsets me whenever I recall it.

YOUNG AND OLD
CALCUTTA, 1998

I must say I've never seen a broken ankle set in such a way. This frail-looking lady looks out from the bamboo and banana leaf bed which she calls home. Beside her sits a wash bowl, a cooking furnace area, a clothes line and a basket full of coal — all she has to sustain her life. We need to do all we can to prevent the next generation — perhaps even some of those who ran to be involved in this photograph — from being condemned to these sort of conditions.

CRICKETERS IN A FOREIGN LAND

RIVER OF LIFE
CALCUTTA, 1998

The Ganges is the source of life for everything that surrounds it. Many depend upon it directly for a wide variety of uses. On one walk along the banks of this cloudy-brown waterway with Gavin Robertson, we came across some locals going about everyday chores, such as washing their cooking utensils and attending to personal hygiene.

The young boy adopting the Muhammad Ali 'pose' in front of Robbo's camera (page 183) was impossible to shake after we gave him a few rupees for performing a couple of swan dives into the murky depths.

Not long after this photo was taken we were swamped by locals and had to make a swift exit to the waiting taxi to avoid being mobbed.

THE ROAD TOLL

NEW DELHI, 1996

Each day, as we travelled to the Feroz Shah Kotla Ground during the only Test of our tour to India in 1996, we came across this outrageous billboard at one of the main traffic intersections. The almost macabre scoreboard was being updated each day, with the previous 24 hours' worth of fatalities creating a new grand total. Having been to numerous countries in my travels, I can fully understand why the road toll is so astronomically high in Delhi. There is only one road rule and that is 'the biggest goes first'.

THE PATIALA EXPRESS
NEW DELHI TO PATIALA, 1996

Some might say it was gamesmanship. Others might suggest we were stitched up. Either way, we certainly had a life experience as we prepared for our one-off Test match in New Delhi in October by travelling by rail for the one warm-up game we'd been allotted. First up, the scheduled four-hour train trip to and fro' Patiala turned into six-and-a-half hours each way. To make matters even less impressive, we'd been told it was a pleasant journey with excellent sightseeing along the way, so we weren't thrilled to find the windows were covered in dirt and grime which made it impossible to see anything outside the train for the entire trip.

Trying to make the most of a tough situation, Slats decided to work on his music technique, both verbally and physically, as we meandered our way to Patiala. In fact, he penned a nice little number entitled 'All Aboard the Patiala Express' which will be his first chart stopper when he hits the big time. Meanwhile, Pistol tried to pretend his crooning fellow passenger wasn't really there as he caught up on the sports news from home.

BREAKFAST OF SORTS
PATIALA, 1996

When we finally arrived after the first half of our train journey from hell, worse was to await us in the form of our hotel. There was no hot water for the four days we were there, no air-conditioning, no pillows that didn't feel like lumps of concrete, no mini-bars. A permanent smell of wet socks lingered in the air. The breakfast was useless to those who didn't possess a cast-iron constitution.

Amid these trying circumstances, we decided to gather each morning in the team room and demolish our supply of muesli bars and vegemite, washed down with some tea and coffee. Mind you, this wasn't bad from a team-bonding aspect.

But that was all!

The guys in the photograph are (left to right): Errol Alcott, Geoff Marsh, Mark Waugh, Jason Gillespie, Mark Taylor and Damien Fleming.

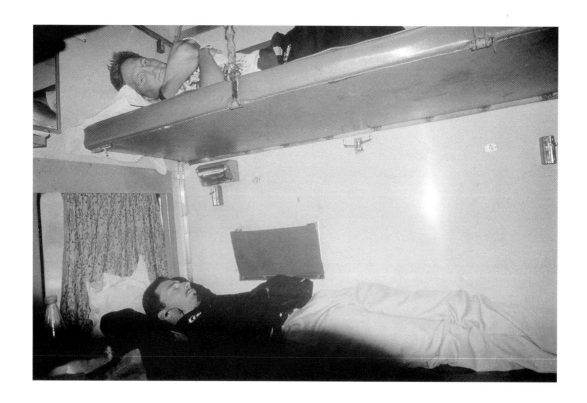

ANOTHER SLOW-MOVING TRAIN
PATIALA TO NEW DELHI, 1996

Not a great way to prepare for a Test match, travelling on a train for six-and-a-half hours each way, but the boys tried to make the best out of a tough situation. The bumpy ride didn't seem to affect Flemo, but his choice of music (Iron Maiden, Megadeth, Kiss etc) had probably altered his state of mind anyway. Heals, meanwhile, doesn't look overly impressed with his lodgings.

ANOTHER DAY
CALCUTTA, 1998

On the fringes of Barrackpore Colony people live in cramped conditions spending plenty of time sitting around with not much to do. My untimely visit down this alleyway caught the mother of this family in the process of grooming herself.

FEEDING TIME
NEW DELHI, 1998

I visit zoos during cricket tours because I find the peaceful atmosphere therapeutic, so I was a little stressed, but at the same time amused, by the sight of these boys continually poking and prodding the monkeys, and also offering them a well-balanced diet of bananas and sandwiches.

Perhaps they hadn't noticed the warning sign?

Steve Waugh's 'Coffin'

Bombay, 1986

Our tour of India in '86 was notable for many extraordinary things, including the second Tied Test in cricket history.

Our captain Allan Border had been the only player to have toured India before, so none of the other lads knew quite what lay in wait for them. For some, it was only a matter of days before the dreaded 'Delhi Belly' struck and by the seventh week of the tour only AB and I still had a clean bill of health. The guys lacked an immunity against the local bugs that infiltrate the water and food, while things weren't helped by the lack of amenities in many of the 'up-country' hotels that had accommodated us.

As I was feeling pretty pleased with my constitution, I rewarded myself with a chocolate milkshake from the counter of the world-class Taj Hotel in Bombay. However, by early the next morning (which, catastrophically for me, was also the opening day of the third and final Test match) I was feeling a tad queasy and a little flushed in the face. As I hoped it might only be a 24-hour thing, I took my place in the line-up, but from almost the instant we began our first innings on the opening morning, I knew I was in serious trouble.

That fluttery, 'butterflies' sensation in my stomach rapidly developed into a buffalo stampede. In the 10 or so minutes before my arrival at the batting crease I visited the toilet no fewer than six times, leaving me a shell of a man when I finally stumbled out to the middle. My brief innings of 6 was the only action I saw all game, apart from a foiled attempt at fielding on the third day when continuous dizzy spells forced me back to the sanctuary of my hotel room for another round of needles.

It took me at least 12 months to fully recover from the stomach bug, which continued to control my bodily functions during that period. However, I wasn't the only one — many others took long periods to readjust to life back home.

This photo of my mock headstone was taken by Simon 'Sniffer' Davis, who was also responsible for the artwork. Back where I lay in my hotel room, there were moments when a burial didn't feel like such a far-fetched possibility.

The sign stuck above my gear and kitbag in the Aussie dressing-room read:

Stephen Waugh

R.I.P.

Born June 2nd, 1965

Died October 17th, 1986

A victim of the dreaded

BOMBAY BELLY

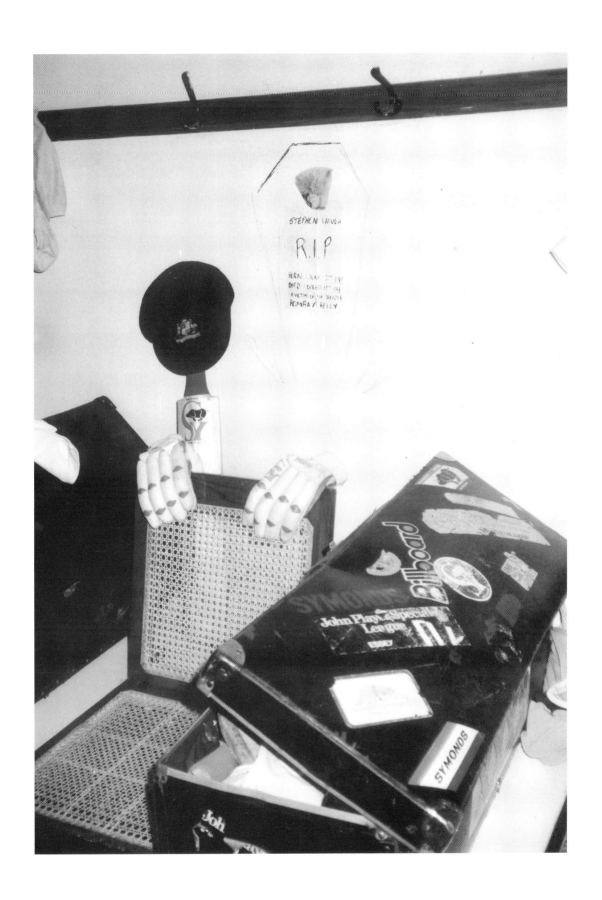

CRICKETERS IN A FOREIGN LAND

DAMIEN FLEMING
COCHIN, 1998

By the time we reached Cochin, five weeks into our tour of India, Flemo had finally had enough of me sticking my camera in his face. So he reversed roles, as we settled into our new hotel just moments after being greeted by a couple of colourful elephants in the hotel's reception area.

AUTOGRAPH HUNTERS
CALCUTTA, 1998

Playing in the Test at Eden Gardens in front of 80,000 fans was a memorable experience, but I will always remember it as a game in which we played probably our worst Test-match cricket for five or six years and a strained groin possibly cost me a hundred (I was run out for 80 in our first innings while batting with a runner).

Being injured in Calcutta means sitting on the sidelines in close proximity to the crowd, so it was only a matter of time before a large group gathered up against the fence, pleading for an autograph. Sensing the possibility of a stampede, the local police asked me not to sign anything, but my shake of the head only made the fans even more determined. Out of nowhere, a sign was suddenly thrust against the fence: 'Why Steve aren't you giving us autograph?'

As they'd made such an effort, I asked a couple of security guards to go over and collect their books. And within seconds of their requests being satisfied, another sign appeared, which said simply: 'Thankyou Steve.'

A CHANCE AT LIFE

UDAYAN BOYS HOME
CALCUTTA, 1998

They say that out of something bad you can always find something good. I've also learnt to try to make sure that something positive comes out of anything negative. Well, I certainly thought of both of these things on the day after we were hammered by India in four days in the Second Test of our series there in 1998.

On the evening of that awful loss in Calcutta, I wandered into my hotel room feeling somewhat dejected and sorry for myself. But that attitude was about to change quite dramatically. Under the door was an envelope containing a letter that caught my attention. It offered me an opportunity to visit some charity organisations, in particular a rehabilitation centre for the sons of leprosy sufferers.

The tone of the letter, from a Mrs Shamlu Dujeda, was one of desperation. The program she was backing was in dire need of funds and volunteer support to keep it functioning. So, having been given an unexpected day off by Tendulkar and co., I decided to visit these boys the next day at their new home, called Udayan, about two hours out of the centre of Calcutta.

The project had started back in 1968 when an Englishman, the Rev. James Stevens, took 11 boys out of a leper colony in order to give them a chance at life. In India, then and now, leprosy is a very misunderstood disease; it not only creates prejudices against the person affected but also stigmatises the whole family. For children whose parents suffer from leprosy, the disease may as well also be theirs because they are ostracised by the community, given no chance at school and left to a shameful existence in the slums, begging for rupees.

From the Rev. Stevens' initial intake the number of boys at Udayan has now grown to over 250, all of whom receive medication if needed, schooling, food, shelter and, most importantly, a new self-belief and self-respect to help them grow as individuals.

The cricket bat you see among the boys in the photograph opposite was, in fact, the only piece of sporting equipment they owned when I visited in April. Funds are always scarce and, quite rightly, health, food, shelter and education must come first.

The entire day was an eye-opener for me, one I'll never forget. First, there was the visit to Udayan, where I was shown around buildings that were simple and built to achieve their objective rather than be anything flashy. The atmosphere in which the boys were being brought up appeared to make them all very happy and content, which was in direct contrast to my next stop.

Just 10 minutes down the road, I arrived at the Barrackpore leper colony where many of the boys I had just seen had begun their lives. The contrast was almost overwhelming, with kids running wild and things such as no sewerage, no electricity, no grassed areas and no running water adding up to living conditions that would be totally unacceptable for most of the world's population. Sitting inside musty, smelly jail cells called homes were the victims of leprosy, a completely avoidable disease if medicine and life education were only available.

I can understand why people don't want to go near a leper colony, because it is a daunting experience seeing rotting flesh, open wounds and deformed hands and feet. However, even though these scenes were confronting and shocking, what captured my attention was the warmth and inner strength of these people, who had obviously suffered more than anyone could imagine — both physically and mentally — yet still retained a positive outlook on life.

I left these people feeling great sorrow, but also comforted by the fact that the boys still in the colony had a chance to get out of the vicious circle ... thanks to Udayan.

While on my drive home a further problem was explained to me, one that Mrs Dujeda hoped I might be able to help with. India is a society where men are traditionally the breadwinners and the head of the family, and consequently it had been the boys who had been given all the chances of rehabilitation, in preference to girls facing the same horrible situation. Having seen how successful the work had been with the boys, a pressing need now existed for a girls' wing to be established.

I needed very little persuasion and quickly agreed to become the patron of the Udayan Girls Wing. That was in March. I've since been back to Calcutta to do some fundraising and, together with support from people in Australia, we've managed to raise around $100,000 so far, enough for the project to begin. Additionally, my sponsors, Gunn & Moore, generously supplied a couple of kitbags full of gear, which allows the boys at Udayan the chance to keep alive their dreams of one day making the Indian side.

The short-term goal for our project is, of course, to get the facilities up and running and to welcome the first intake of girls. But the bigger objective is to educate people about leprosy and to help eradicate a disease that is so easy to prevent if it's diagnosed early.

A CHANCE AT LIFE

THE EYES HAVE IT

UDAYAN, 1998

Saying goodbye to the boys of Udayan wasn't easy ... largely because I couldn't shut the door of our vehicle. Cameras and cricketers are an instant cure for shyness and the lads swarmed around me to say goodbye.

WELCOME
CALCUTTA, 1998

A look of desperation covers this woman's face as, almost embarrassingly but still warmly, she welcomes me into her home. Sadly, her 'dwelling' has literally been put together from bits and pieces collected from the street.

FAMILY SUPPORT
CALCUTTA, 1998

A father proudly shows off his son, while his daughter watches. Just like the photograph on page 195, the family members are obviously delighted to be with each other. Unfortunately, in both cases the ravages of leprosy have taken away most of the fathers' physical powers, but still their warmth and strength are an inspiration — to me and, I'm sure, to their children, too.

BARRACKPORE COLONY
CALCUTTA, 1998

I'm standing with three of the elderly leprosy sufferers and a boy hopeful of gaining admittance to Udayan. Many of these people not only lose their fingers and toes, but their eyesight can also be badly affected.

MOTHER AND SON

CALCUTTA, 1998

This woman is happy to stand with her son for this image because she realises that any publicity might raise awareness of their plight and give the children who live around her a much better life.

MOTHER AND DAUGHTER
CALCUTTA, 1998

A healthy girl watches over her 39-year-old mother, who proudly shows us her knitting skills despite her apparent handicaps. The tragedy of this situation, which her mother would be well aware of, is that if this young girl doesn't get out of her current environment she will be forced to either go out onto the streets to beg for money to support her family or, more disastrously, turn to the wretched life of a street prostitute.

HOWZAT!!
CALCUTTA, 1998

It's amazing! No matter how poor and seemingly deprived one is in India, international cricketers from all over the world are recognised wherever they go. When I visited the leper colony at Barrackpore, the kids were quickly mimicking the matches they'd seen glimpses of and feverishly asking about heroes such as Tendulkar and Azharuddin.

The youngster (right) giving me the pointed appeal had just sent down an imaginary thunderbolt from Javagal Srinath, India's paceman who had such a successful series against us in 1998. He quite clearly thinks he's trapped me plumb in front!

Moments later, a fence paling and a tennis ball were located and a game began in earnest, with yours truly copping a barrage of short stuff — much to the delight of all the families in the compound.

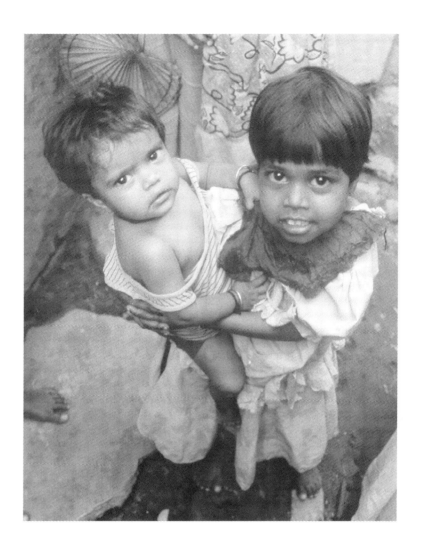

FACES IN THE CROWD
CALCUTTA, 1998

Children in the slum certainly grow up before their time, taking on responsibilities that would seem totally inappropriate in our society. This young girl of no more than five years of age is burdened with the task of caring for her younger sister for most of the day, while her parents try to make enough money to put food in their's and their children's mouths each day.

THE POWER OF PRAYER
UDAYAN, 1998

If you compare the meagre pickings available on the streets and alleyways to the nourishment served up three times a day at Udayan, you quickly realise that these boys have every reason to feel blessed. Here they are giving thanks for a dinner that awaits them in the food hall.

The main meal usually consists of a large spoonful of rice, lentils and dhal, which gives the boys a rich source of protein and carbohydrates to keep them strong and healthy.

ON THE EDGE
CALCUTTA, 1998

Like too many children of Calcutta who are obliged to endure living conditions unimaginable to people in the western world, girls such as these are forced to grow up so fast that their childhoods are sacrificed for the sake of survival.

Without any real education, many girls from Barrackpore Colony are sent to work, or to beg for money, while still being expected to look after their younger brothers and sisters. This was why I was enticed to become patron of the campaign for a girls wing to be established at Udayan. The girls in this photograph, which was taken in a lane just metres from the colony, are perfect candidates for this project.

As I was guided through the compound, I could easily measure the success of Udayan. The pleas from parents, desperate for their children to be involved in the next intake, told the story.

TEAM PHOTO
UDAYAN, 1998

This photograph was taken in front of one of the buildings that each house and sleep around 65 boys. At present, they still sleep on concrete floors with a hessian bag — but this is still 100 times better than what they would have been facing in the past. In time, one hopes a suitable sponsor can be found that will allow each of the boys, and the girls who will soon be living there, too, the luxury of a bed and a pillow.